WAR, PEACE,
and
THE BIBLE

WAR, PEACE,

and

THE BIBLE

J. CARTER SWAIM

ORBIS BOOKS
Maryknoll, New York 10545

The Catholic Foreign Mission Society of America (Maryknoll) recruits and trains people for overseas missionary service. Through Orbis Books Maryknoll aims to foster the international dialogue that is essential to mission. The books published, however, reflect the opinions of their authors and are not meant to represent the official position of the society.

Copyright © 1982 by Orbis Books, Maryknoll, NY 10545

Manufactured in the United States of America

Manuscript editor: Lisa McGaw

Library of Congress Cataloging in Publication Data

Swaim, J. Carter (Joseph Carter), 1904-
  War, peace, and the Bible.

  Includes bibliographical references and index.
  1. Christianity and war 2. Peace (Theology)
I. Title.
BT736.2.S94   261.8'73   81-16889
ISBN 0-88344-752-5 (pbk.)   AACR2

To
Carl and Mildred
Soule

Makárioi hoi eirēnopoioí

CONTENTS

ABBREVIATIONS

Scripture quotations are from the Revised Standard Version of the Bible, copyrighted 1946, 1952, 1971, 1973 unless they are credited otherwise.

JCS	J. Carter Swaim
M	Moffatt
NAB	New American Bible
NEB	New English Bible

Preface

To translate the Scriptures into the speech of fourth-century Goths, Ulfilas, bishop of the Goths, had to invent an alphabet—the first of hundreds of similar contributions that missionaries have made to world culture and understanding. Because the people to whom he ministered were so fierce and undisciplined, Ulfilas refrained from translating certain warlike portions of the Old Testament. "In this matter," he explained, "my people need the bit rather than the bridle."

Another early Bible translation followed an exactly opposite course. Aelfric, a Benedictine monk considered the outstanding English prose stylist around A.D. 1000, made an Anglo-Saxon version of parts of the Bible, including Joshua, Judges, portions of the books of Kings, and Maccabees. The reason he bore down heavily upon these warlike portions of the Old Testament was his desire to kindle patriotic fervor among his fellows and so arouse them to resist the invading Danes.

In colonial America, the Moravians came to Georgia and began to evangelize the Cherokee Indians. Under the tutelage of missionaries, Sequoya reduced the Cherokee tongue to writing. Soon parts of the Bible were printed in the syllabary Sequoya had devised. Before distributing the version widely, the sponsors presented a copy to the Cherokee chief and asked his approval. After careful study, his verdict was: "Plenty good book! Strange thing: white man have it so long and be so bad."

Does the Bible teach war or peace? These historical incidents demonstrate that both are there to be found. The question is, which are we to believe and follow today? To answer that, we must recall the way the Bible came into being. It did not, like Athena, spring full-grown from the head of Zeus, nor was it handed down from heaven with the name of a Bible society stamped on the cover.

Instead, it represents God's self-revelation across many centuries. An early Christian writer, addressing himself to those of Hebrew background, put it thus: "Bit by bit and through many media God spoke in olden times to our fathers; now in these last days he has spoken to us through One who is a Son" (Heb. 1:1f., JCS). The revelation was bit by bit—that is to say, a portion at a time, not all at once, suddenly and overwhelmingly.

With regard to families, for example, we can easily recognize development within the Bible. Torah provides that anyone who strikes father or mother or curses parents shall be put to death (cf. Exod. 21:15, 17; Lev. 20:9). Parents who deemed a son stubborn and unruly could have him stoned to death by the community (cf. Deut. 21:20). No one now holds that God teaches child abuse. When persons were to be ransomed, a higher money value was placed upon men and boys than upon women and girls (cf. Lev. 27:1–7). If a bride was found not to be virgin, "the men of her city shall stone her to death" (Deut. 22:20ff.). No one now holds the belief that God advocates male chauvinism.

Not only was revelation "bit by bit." It was also a multimedia event: vision, audition, theophany. In a dream of the night, Jacob learned that a ladder might be "pitched between Heaven and Charing Cross" (cf. Gen. 28:10–17 and Francis Thompson's poem "In No Strange Land"). In a youthful crisis of vocation, Isaiah (6:8) heard a voice: "Whom shall I send, and who will go for us?" In such experiences, the senses—sight, sound, taste—were strangely mingled. The author of Revelation 1:12 can say, "I turned to see the voice that was speaking." Ezekiel, confronted with words upon a scroll, says, "Then I ate it; and it was in my mouth as sweet as honey" (3:1–3).

Not only did revelation come through such divine entrance into human personality, but God's disclosures came also through insights that dawned upon those undergoing ordinary human experiences: a poet awed at the wonder of the Palestinian night; a man watching earthenware vessels being fashioned upon a potter's wheel; a herdsman contemplating a basket of summer fruit.

Revelation came, too, through more poignant personal experiences: a king's concubine, mourning the death of the two sons she had borne him, keeping watch over their fallen bodies until "God heeded supplication for the land" (cf. 2 Sam. 21:8–14); a woman long barren blessed with childbirth and praising God: "He raises up the poor from the dust; he lifts the needy from the ashheap" (1 Sam. 2:8); a long-suffering husband whose wife's unfaithfulness led him to comtemplate the love that would not let him go.

The question is not whether God has spoken through the Scripture, but, rather, what God's last word is. Of old there was the law, administered by the priests; the mature counsels of wise men; oracles spoken by prophets. But God's last word is Jesus. Wars in the Old Testament do not mean that God teaches us in these days that national policy should revolve around armaments that deprive the poor of bread, nor depend upon weapons capable of wiping out the human race. If Deborah can sing, "The Lord is a man of war," the early church could proclaim of Jesus, "He is our peace."

The prophet believed that Messiah would be Prince of Peace. Of One whose words were full of grace and truth, God said, "This is my beloved Son. Hear him." The letter to the Hebrews insists (7:18f.) that in Jesus "a former commandment is set aside because of its weakness and uselessness (for the law made nothing perfect); on the other hand, a better hope is introduced, through which we draw near to God."

If we read the Bible in that way, we may find ourselves paraphrasing the Cherokee chieftain when first he looked into the Scriptures: "Plenty good book. Strange thing: 'Christian' man have it so long and be so warlike."

WAR, PEACE,
and
THE BIBLE

1

Yahweh Is a Man of War

The Chosen People were assigned a land that Ezekiel (5:5) thought was "in the center of the nations." Other countries, too—China and Greece, for example—have believed themselves at the center of the world. We all succumb to the egocentric fallacy: we are *here*; everyone else is out there somewhere. No place on the surface of a globe can ever be described as its center. Yet the Hebrews had a better claim than most. Jerusalem *is* midway between North Cape and the Cape of Good Hope. Moreover, it is midway between San Francisco and Vladivostok!

This land at the center of things was already occupied by people whose worship involved human sacrifice, sexual orgies, and other bizarre practices. Following the liberation from Egypt and successful escape across the Red Sea, Moses and his people chanted, "I will sing to the Lord, for he has triumphed gloriously; the horse and his rider he has thrown into the sea. . . . The Lord is a man of war" (Exod. 15:1,3). With that as background, it was inevitable that, upon entering the Land of Promise, Joshua and his cohorts should assume that the way to wipe out idolatry was to wipe out idolaters.

Consequently, on their way to the Land of Promise, the Hebrews carried out drastic extermination. When Sihon, king of Heshbon, refused to allow free passage through his territory, "we seized all his cities and doomed them all with their men, women and children; we left no survivor" (Deut. 2:34, NAB). Similarly with Og, king of Bashan: "We defeated him so completely that we left him no survivor" (Deut. 3:3, NAB). Following victory over

1

a coalition of Midianite kings, the Hebrews "took captive the women of Midian and their little ones; and they took as booty all their cattle, their flocks, and all their goods" and "set on fire all the towns where they had settled and all their encampments" (Num. 31:9f.). Infuriated at this, Moses ordered them to kill all the women and boys, but to "keep for yourselves all girls who had no intercourse with a man" (Num. 31:18, NAB).

Moses once ordered the sword unsheathed against his own people. Learning that, in his absence, Aaron had fashioned a golden calf and proclaimed it to be a god, Moses summoned loyalists to gather round him and said, "Put your sword on your hips . . .! Now go up and down the camp, from gate to gate, and slay your own kinsmen, your friends and neighbors. . . . That day there fell about three thousand of the people" (Exod. 32:27f. NAB). One might well ask whether Moses had read the Ten Commandments he had just brought down from Sinai.

The Conquest and Settlement of Canaan

The conquest of Canaan began with a spy story that bears no more relation to reality than did the report that the Central Intelligence Agency (CIA) made to President Jimmy Carter about the Shah of Iran. Having gone over to spy out the land, the Hebrew secret service reported that it was "a land that devours its inhabitants; and all the people that we saw in it are men of great stature" (Num. 13:32). It was inhabited by giants so big that "we seemed to ourselves like grasshoppers, and so we seemed to them" (Num. 13:33). According to Deuteronomy 1:28 (NAB), "Our kinsmen have made us faint-hearted by reporting that the people are stronger and taller than we, and their cities are large and fortified to the sky."

When Joshua was able to muster enough courage to continue, he and his troops found that Canaanites were not ten feet tall. After a week of marching around the city and blowing trumpets, the walls of Jericho came tumbling down. Thereupon the Hebrews "utterly destroyed all in the city, both men and women, young and old, oxen, sheep, and asses, with the edge of the sword" (Josh. 6:21). By trickery and ambush, they "utterly destroyed all the inhabitants of Ai," and burned the city, making it forever "a heap of ruins" (Josh. 8:26, 28).

They attacked Hazor, too: "every man they smote with the edge of the sword, until they had destroyed them, and they did not leave any that breathed" (Josh. 11:14). Similarly, they smote "the inhabitants of Jabesh-gilead with the edge of the sword; also the women and the little ones" (Judg. 21:10); and they reveled in the spoils of war (cf. Deut. 20:14). The command sometimes was: "you shall not leave a single soul alive" (Deut. 20:16, NAB; cf. 1 Sam. 15:8; 27: 9, 11).

Horrible as all this sounds, it was not warfare in the modern sense. Weapons were not nearly as fierce as those devised in more "enlightened" days, nor did they spread such devastation. "After other wars, it was possible for nations to dig themselves out of the rubble. After a nuclear war, even the rubble contains the seeds of death."[1] Old Testament wars were far from total. Thus, in spite of all the violence the invaders were able to muster, idolatry was not wiped out; the Canaanite cities continued to be inhabited (cf. Judg. 1:19–32) and the struggle for pure religion continued. Each tribe was allotted its territory, but all found they had somehow to coexist with pagan neighbors.

Numbers 31:7 tells how Moses' troops waged war against the Midianites "and slew every male," and subsequently took captive all the women and boys (31:7ff.), then set fire to all their towns. In the time of Gideon, however, Midianite raiders still harassed: "Israel was reduced to misery by Midian" (Judg. 6:6, NAB). As late as the time of the monarchy, the settlers were still contending with many besides the Philistines. ". . . Joshua mowed down Amalek and his people with the edge of the sword" (Exod. 17:13). Much later, Saul "defeated the Amalekites . . . and utterly destroyed all the people with the edge of the sword" (1 Sam. 15:7f.) The relatively mild nature of these exploits is suggested by the fact that the families of the soldiers prepared food and took it to them (cf. 1 Sam. 17:17). In Indochina in modern times, Annamese soldiers wanted to be accompanied by their families, but the Western nations regarded this as quite uncivilized.

Among the Hebrews, too, there were efforts to make war more "humane." Certain classes of citizens were exempt from participation. A man who had built a new house could stay at home and move in. A man who had planted a vineyard could remain and enjoy the fruit (cf. Deut. 20:5f.) "When a man is newly married, he shall not go out with the army or be charged with any business; he shall be free at home one year, to be happy with his wife" (Deut. 24:5). Even those who had no stomach for it were not required to go: "What man is there who is fearful and fainthearted? Let him go back to his house, lest the heart of his fellows melt as his heart" (Deut. 20:8). Hebrew selective service thus differed from that of some neighbors. Herodotus tells that under Darius and Xerxes the Persians permitted no exemption.

Among the Hebrews there was also a quite modern concern about the environment. We know that military deforestation has wrought havoc on the earth, vastly increasing the acreage that has become desert and imperiling humanity's oxygen supply. Hebrew troops were not allowed to harm the forests: "When you besiege a city . . . you shall not destroy its trees. . . . Are the trees in the field men that they should be besieged by you?" (Deut. 20:19). We can see from all this how "uncivilized" warfare was in those pre-atomic days.

For all the violence employed in overcoming the Canaanites, the Hebrew occupation did not wipe out pagan religious practices. Instead, the Hebrews took over some of their abominations, perhaps even the notion that God is a man of war. To cite that phrase no more proves that Yahweh was a battle god than it proves that he was a man. Archaeologists have turned up bronze images of the Canaanite Baal brandishing a sword. Perhaps in addressing people who thought in such terms, the Hebrews pictured their deity, too, as one who was no Casper Milquetoast.

The sword is often referred to as a symbol of divine authority. When our first parents were banished from the Garden, God "placed . . . a flaming sword which turned every way, to guard the way to the tree of life" (Gen. 3:24). Balaam's "ass saw the angel of the Lord standing in the road, with a drawn sword in his hand" (Num. 22:23; cf. 22:31). David, intending to take a census—apparently for the purpose of assessing military capabilities—"saw the angel of the Lord standing between earth and heaven, and in his hand a drawn sword stretched out over

Jerusalem" (1 Chron. 21:16), suggesting that preparation for war would have a devastating effect upon the king's own land. There followed pestilence, the building of altars, the presentation of burnt offerings. "Then the Lord commanded the angel; and he put his sword back into its sheath" (1 Chron. 21:27).

God and Warfare

Even so, the Hebrews appear to have modified the concept of God as ruthless force. Far more common than "man of war" to describe the Eternal is "Lord of hosts," described by David as "God of the armies of Israel" (1 Sam. 17:45). But "Lord of hosts" has another—and broader—meaning. It was anciently supposed that the heavenly realm was organized in the same way as the earthly, and the celestial bodies—sun, moon, and stars— came to be thought of as heaven's army. The warlike Song of Deborah proclaims: "From heaven fought the stars, from their courses they fought against Sisera" (Judg. 5:20). So far from being a strictly military term, the phrase "Lord of hosts" could be interpreted as a confession that God is above the fray, not on any one side. It thus "sums up the Israelite faith that Yahweh alone is Lord in heaven and on earth."[2]

Still, the Hebrews continued to be influenced by the people among whom they dwelled. This was true to such an extent that Ezekiel (16:45 NAB) dared to call in question the legitimacy of his people's ancestry: "Your mother was a Hittite and your father an Amorite."

One of the more hideous Canaanite customs was child sacrifice (cf. 2 Kings 3:26f.). Through the experience with his own son at Mount Moriah (cf. Gen. 22:2–12), Abraham learned that God did not require human sacrifice. Yet the Hebrews in Canaan sometimes followed the practice, which appears to have been at least partially institutionalized by Solomon. On the mountain east of Jerusalem he built an altar to the Moabite god Chemosh (cf. 1 Kings 11:7), which was abolished by Josiah (cf. 2 Kings 23:13). The king of Moab, finding himself in desperate straits, "took his eldest son who was to reign in his stead, and offered him for a burnt offering" (2 Kings 3:27). According to 2 Kings 16:2f., King

Ahaz followed suit: "He even burned his son as an offering, according to the abominable practices of the nations" that had been in Canaan before the Hebrews came.

During Hoshea's nine-year reign over Israel, according to 2 Kings 17, the Assyrians came, captured Samaria, and "carried the Israelites away to Assyria" (vs. 6). This fate came upon them because, among other things, "they burned their sons and their daughters as offerings" (vs. 17). This appears to have been rationalized upon the basis of Exodus 22:29: "The first-born of your sons you shall give to me." Ezekiel 20:26 represents this as one of the ways in which God disciplined his people: "I defiled them through their very gifts in making them offer by fire all their firstborn, that I might horrify them; I did it that they might know that I am the Lord."

Isaiah 57:5 reveals that the practice was not unknown even in postexilic times. One of the hateful things for which the nation is rebuked is "[you] slay your children in the valleys." Jeremiah 7:31 makes it clear that this was a misunderstanding of God's intention: "they have built the high place of Topheth, which is in the valley of the son of Hinnom, to burn their sons and their daughters in the fire; which I did not command, nor did it come into my mind." The valley of the son of Hinnom originally marked the boundary between the tribes of Judah and Benjamin. The ritual cremation carried out there led to its being called "valley of Slaughter" (Jer. 7:31ff.; 19:5ff.), and gave birth to the notion of the hell of fire, the Gehenna of which Jesus spoke.

Manasseh, son of the good king Hezekiah, reigned for fifty-five years, and "did what was evil in the sight of the Lord. . . . He burned his son as an offering" and did other wicked things (2 Kings 21:2, 6). In 2 Kings 21:13ff. is disclosed the punishment Manasseh thus brought upon his nation: " '. . . I will wipe Jerusalem as one wipes a dish . . . and give them into the hand of their enemies.' . . . Manasseh shed very much innocent blood, till he had filled Jerusalem from one end to another." Manasseh, old and full of wicked days, "humbled himself greatly before the God of his fathers. He prayed to him, and God . . . heard his supplication" (2 Chron. 33:12f.). The Chronicler gives no account of his petition, but the Apocrypha include the Prayer of Manasseh, in which he pleads, "I am rejected because of my sin, and I have no relief" (vs. 10). He hopes, nevertheless, that the compassionate and long-suffering God will forgive and "not destroy me with my transgressions" (vs. 13).

George Adam Smith says that Micah 6:8 is "the greatest saying of the Old Testament, . . . an ideal of religion to which no subsequent century has ever been able to add either grandeur or tenderness."[3] It is not often noticed that this is set in contrast with history's most hideous misrepresentation of what it is God requires, the offering up of children: " 'With what shall I come before the Lord, . . . shall I give my first-born for my transgression, the fruit of my body for the sin of my soul?' He has showed you, O man, what is good, and what does the Lord require of you but to do justice, and to love kindness, and to walk humbly with your God?" (Mic. 6:6–8).

There are passages in the prophets that continue to speak of God as one who wields a sword. "I will make many peoples appalled at you . . . when I brandish my sword before them" (Ezek. 32:10). "I will brandish your sons, O Zion, . . . and wield you like a warrior's sword" (Zech. 9:13). Having already "drunk its fill in the heavens," God's sword descends upon the wicked nations that suppose he demands slaughter rather than justice: "The Lord has a sword; it is sated with blood, it is gorged with fat" (Isa. 34:5f.). "The Lord goes forth like a mighty man, like a man of war he stirs up his fury; . . . he shows himself mighty against his foes" (Isa. 42:13).

Under the monarchy, war became for Israel an instrument of national policy, the king declaring it at will. Even the prophet Elijah, to wipe out Baalism, seized the prophets of Baal, "brought them down to the brook Kishon, and killed them there" (1 Kings 18:40). Over this he apparently did not grieve. What he does lament is that his own people have "thrown down thy altars, and slain thy prophets with the sword" (1 Kings 19:10; cf. 19: 14).

Since war for Israel was a holy thing, the priests were expected to accompany the armies into battle, taking with them the ark, the visible symbol of God's invincible presence (cf. 1 Sam. 4:4; 30:7; cf. also Num. 31:6; 2 Sam. 11:11). There was another factor now to be reckoned with. Under the monarchy, God was no longer king. He spoke his mind through the prophets, who no longer

sanctioned every military venture as holy war. So far from proclaiming that God was on Israel's side, the prophets declared that
Yahweh was turning military forces against his people in order to
judge them for their sins. The prophets saw, too, that Yahweh was
bringing a redemption that transcended all nationalistic hopes:
"the Lord of hosts . . . is your Redeemer, the God of the whole
earth" (Isa. 54:5). So far from sanctioning war, a psalmist (Ps.
46:9) affirmed that the God of Israel "makes wars cease to the end
of the earth."

Psalm 24:7–10 is an antiphonal chant, used when the people
approach the sanctuary. Halting at the gate of the temple, they
sing, " . . . be lifted up, O ancient doors! that the King of glory
may come in. Who is the King of glory? The Lord, strong and
mighty, the Lord, mighty in battle! . . . The Lord of hosts, he is
the King of glory!" Some think this celebrates God's work at creation, when he won a great battle over the dragon of chaos (cf. Ps.
74:12–17). In any case, the phrase "Lord of hosts" has taken on
new meaning. It is no longer a battle cry but a prayer that the God
of creation may open the gates of the temple for all who come to
worship (cf. Isa. 44:6; 45:13; 47:4; 48:20; 51:15).

David was a man of war. By waging it almost incessantly, he
created an empire, triumphing over the Philistines, Moabites,
Syrians, Edomites, Ammonites (cf. 2 Sam. 8). Psalm 144 represents David as giving thanks for the skill he possessed as a warrior: "Blessed be the Lord . . . who trains my hands for war, and
my fingers for battle" (vs. 1), the latter referring perhaps to "wise
conduct of campaigns" (Prov. 20:18; 24:6). He gives thanks not
only for military skills but also for victories: "my rock . . . and
my deliverer, my shield and he in whom I take refuge, who sub-
dues my people under me" (Ps. 144:2, mg.).

It was prowess of this kind that made David Israel's great
hero—and the Star of David is modern Israel's emblem. The
Bible's final judgment upon the great warrior is of a vastly different nature. David, who has captured the ark from the Philistines, made and fortified Jerusalem as his capital, and made the
nations fear him, wishes to crown his reign by building a magnifi-
cent house of worship. God's judgment is that such a man, in spite
of personal charm and poetic skill, is not worthy of such a purpose. "I made preparations for building," says David in pathetic

farewell. "But God said to me, 'You may not build a house for my name, for you are a warrior and have shed blood' " (1 Chron. 28:2f.). Solomon was permitted to build a temple, but "neither hammer nor axe nor any tool of iron"—the metal used for instruments of war—"was heard in the temple while it was being built (1 Kings 6:7).

Among the Hebrews was a little-known prophet who demonstrated that the determination to do justice could turn out to be practical politics. Oded lived at a time when unsound economics, as manifested in the luxury and extravagance of Solomon's court, had led to a division in Hebrew society. The nation had split into north and south. The northern kingdom, with its capital in Samaria, made war upon the southern kingdom, with its capital in Jerusalem. The northerners, under Pekah, won a tremendous victory. In such matters the statistics tend to become exaggerated. The record has it that 120,000 southerners were slain in a single day, and 200,000 taken captive.

The captives and the spoil the victors carried off to Samaria. The army, however, had not reckoned with Oded. In the simple philosophy of the time, he said the southerners had sinned; this was why God allowed them to be defeated. But, he said (2 Chron. 28:9), "you have slain them in a rage which has reached up to heaven." Moreover, two wrongs do not make a right. To those coming home from war he announced, " 'You shall not bring the captives in here, for you propose to bring upon us guilt against the Lord in addition to our present sins and guilt. For our guilt is already great' " (28:13).

Samaria's community officials were evidently reasonable men; Oded's belief in kindness to enemies made sense to them. What they wanted was peace and security, and this appealed to them as a way to get it. So they returned the spoil to the captives and the captives to their homes: "they clothed them, gave them sandals, provided them with food and drink, and anointed them; and carrying all the feeble among them on asses, they brought them to their kinsfolk at Jericho" (28:15).

When the king of Syria was warring against Israel and victory was won at Samaria, the king of Israel said to Elisha, "Shall I slay them?" Setting the pattern Oded was later to follow, Elisha answered emphatically, " 'You shall not slay them. Would you slay those whom you have taken captive with your sword and with your bow? Set bread and water before them, that they may eat and drink and go to their master.' So he prepared for them a great feast." Reporting this novel experiment in peacemaking, the historian adds, "And the Syrians came no more on raids into the land of Israel" (2 Kings 6:11–23).

The Changing Attitude toward War

From the eighth century B.C., the prophets ceased to bless Israel's wars, declaring them to be not holy but rather deserving punishment for the nation's sins. Amos (5:18–20) declares that the better day his people seek by their own might will prove to be "darkness, and not light; . . . gloom with no brightness in it." Better times will come only when citizens "speak the truth to one another, render. . . judgments that are true and make for peace, do not devise evil in [their] hearts" (Zech. 8:16f.); ". . . my servant" says the Lord, " . . . will bring forth justice to the nations" (Isa. 42:1); society must convert weapons of war into tools for peace (cf. Isa. 2:4; Mic. 4:3f.).

The writing prophets were unanimous in their conviction that the day of the Lord's real triumph could never be ushered in through military conquest. Expectations that it could were doomed to disappointment. Isaiah 13:9, 15 says: "Behold, the day of the Lord comes. . . . Whoever is found will be thrust through, and whoever is caught will fall by the sword." "That day is the day of the Lord God of hosts, a day of vengeance, to avenge himself on his foes. The sword shall devour and be sated, and drink its fill of their blood" (Jer. 46:10; cf. 25:33–35).

It is a day when cosmic forces will join to make known God's displeasure at humankind's sin: "A day of wrath is that day, . . . a day of darkness and gloom, a day of clouds and thick darkness, . . . the owl shall hoot in the window, the raven croak on the threshold" (Zeph. 1:15; 2:14). Ezekiel 39:17–20 pictures carrion birds and flesh-eating animals as having a field day: " ' . . . you shall eat fat till you are filled, and drink blood till you are drunk. . . . you shall be filled at my table with horses and riders, with mighty men and all kinds of warriors,' says the Lord God." Joel 2:2 describes the day of the Lord as "a day of darkness and gloom, a day of clouds and thick darkness!" ". . . the day of the Lord is near," says Ezekiel. "It will be a day of clouds, a time of doom for the nations" (30:3).

It was clear from the beginning that war could never bring about the society God intended. As early as the time of Moses, God revealed that wrongdoing would lead to violence and reprisal: "You shall not afflict any widow or orphan. If you do . . . I will kill you with the sword" (Exod. 22:22-24). The same promise is made to the nation as to individuals: "If you walk in my statutes and observe my commandments, . . . I will give peace in the land, . . . and none shall make you afraid; . . . and the sword shall not go through your land" (Lev. 26:3-6).

After the American War between the States, the church historian Philip Schaff returned to his native Europe to help his kindred understand that fratricidal strife. He explained it as God's "judgment on centuries-long complicity by an entire nation in the sin of slavery." So, too, the writing prophets of the Old Testament proclaim that the swords that fall upon Israel or sweep through their cities like a whirlwind (cf. Hos. 11:5f.) are God's judgments upon Israel's sins. One of the sins they specify is idolatry. Among the Hebrews, idolatry was equated with adultery, and the whole nation is accused of having "played the harlot" (Ezek. 23:5-10; 16:35-41).

Among other sins that must be requited by the sword are pride and covetousness; greed for land; the shedding of blood within the community; being unfaithful to God, rebelling against him, or dealing treacherously with him; and a long list of corrupt business practices, such as the infamous false measure, the accursed short bushel, scales that deceive, and a bag of light weights: "they sell honest folk for money, the needy for a pair of shoes; they trample down the poor like dust" (Amos 2:6f.,M); "coveting fields and seizing them, coveting houses and snatching them" (Mic. 2:2, M); "judges passing verdicts for a bribe, priests pattering oracles for pay" (Mic. 3:11, M).

Enterprising businessmen wish to turn the Sabbath day into a market day, muttering, "When will the sabbath be done, that our corn may be on sale?" (Amos 8:5, M). For the prophet of Tekoa, one of the most tragic things was that the good people did nothing: "So evil is the time, the prudent keep silent" (Amos 5:13;

compare Smith, *Book of the Twelve Prophets*, 1:169), and the
affluent continued to live extravagantly, "lolling on their ivory
divans, sprawling on their couches, dining off fresh lamb and
fatted veal, crooning to the music of the lute, . . . lapping wine by
the bowlful, and using for ointment the best of the oil—with
never a single thought for the bleeding wounds of the nation"
(Amos 6:4–6, M).

Another transgression was the violation of human rights and
the despising of the Creator of these rights (cf. Joel 3:6–8). Jeremiah hears God say: "You have not obeyed me by proclaiming
liberty, . . . I proclaim to you liberty to the sword, to pestilence,
and to famine" (34:17). Ezékiel (6:11) summarizes the reasons
why Israel became involved in war: "because of all the evil
abominations of the house of Israel . . . they shall fall by the
sword, by famine, and by pestilence." The immediate, practical,
and widespread effect of God's judgment upon the nation's sins
was exile and dispersion: "I will scatter them among the nations
. . . and I will send the sword after them" (Jer. 9:16).

There are terrible pictures, too, of devastation wrought by the
sword. Moses had warned of the catastrophe that conflict could
bring: "In the open the sword shall bereave, and in the chambers
shall be terror, destroying both young man and virgin, the sucking
child with the man of gray hairs" (Deut. 32:25). It transpired even
more tragically than Moses had imagined. Soldiers "ripped up
women with child" (Amos 1:13), and wives turned to harlotry (cf.
Amos 7:17). King Cyrus "tramples kings under foot" and "scat-
ters them with his sword like dust" (Isa. 41:2, NEB). In its train
war brought famine: "Happier were the victims of the sword than
the victims of hunger" (Lam. 4:9) and pillage: "the slain fall in
Egypt, and her wealth is carried away" (Ezek. 30:4).

Recounting what happened after the Babylonians had sacked
Jerusalem, the elegist sobs, "In the dust of the streets lie the young
and the old; my maidens and my young men have fallen by the
sword" (Lam. 2:21). The horror is unspeakable: "every one who
passes by it will be horrified and will hiss because of all its disasters. And I will make them eat the flesh of their sons and their
daughters, and every one shall eat the flesh of his neighbor in the
siege and in the distress" (Jer. 19:8f.).

Citizens compelled to drain the "cup of the wine of wrath . . .

shall drink and stagger and be crazed because of the sword" (Jer. 25:16); they will "be drunk and vomit, fall and rise no more" (Jer. 25:27). "In the street the sword bereaves; in the house it is like death" (Lam. 1:20). Ezekiel has a similar picture: "The sword is without, pestilence and famine are within; he that is in the field dies by the sword; and him that is in the city famine and pestilence devour" (7:15); ". . . every heart will melt and all hands will be feeble, every spirit will faint and all knees will be weak as water" (21:7; cf. 21:14f., 26f.; 31:15ff.; 33:27).

Such visions were seen also in the time of the prophet Habakkuk, whose name apparently means "One who caresses or embraces"—as Jerome said, "either because of his love to the Lord, or because he wrestles with God." Far as the eye can see, Habakkuk's horizon is dark with tyranny and oppression brought about by an evil power, whether Assyria, Egypt, Chaldea, or the Greeks. The prophet's own nation is "thrown into disorder, revelation paralysed, justice perverted" (cf. Hab. 1:3f.). It is not, however, Israel alone that has been afflicted. "The tyrant has outraged humanity"; "the impious are swallowing up the good. . . . Hook them, haul them up, sweep them into the net" (Hab. 1:13, 15, M).[4]

Habakkuk wonders how long this is to continue: "Are they to go on drawing the sword, murdering peoples without pity?" (1:17, M). From his watch-tower the prophet catches a vision: "You impious man! his powers shall fail him; the good man lasts and lives as he is faithful" (2:4, M). His doom is sure. "Tyranny," says George Adam Smith, "is intolerable. In the nature of things it cannot endure, but works out its own penalties. By oppressing so many nations, the tyrant is preparing the instruments of his own destruction. As he treats them, so in time shall they treat him. He is like a debtor who increases the number of his creditors. Some day they shall rise up and exact from him the last penny. . . . In cutting off others he is but forfeiting his own life."[5]

So the taunt-song of Habakkuk continues: "He would sweep all nations in, he would rake in every race. Shall not they all taunt him in chorus, and shout this satire at him?—Woe to him who heaps up plunder (ah, how long!), loading himself with what he must repay! Shall not your victims suddenly arise, and men awake to make you shake?—then you shall be their prey? Many a nation you have harried, so the rest shall harry you, for the blood you shed, for your devastation of earth and every town and nation" (2:5-8, M).

Similarly Isaiah of the Exile (49:25f.) hears God say, "Even the captives of the mighty shall be taken, and the prey of the tyrant rescued, for I will contend with those who contend with you, and I will save your children. I will make your oppressors eat their own flesh, and they shall be drunk with their own blood as with wine. Then all flesh shall know that I am the Lord your Savior, and your Redeemer, the Mighty One of Jacob." Zechariah 11:9 has a different image, equally descriptive of the end result of hatred and conflict: "What is to die, let it die; what is to be destroyed, let it be destroyed; and let those that are left devour the flesh of one another."

What war does to the city and to the countryside is intolerable, but its greatest crime is what it does to domestic life, making it impossible. Among people of the biblical world and, ideally, among people everywhere, there is no joy comparable to that of a family dwelling in peace and security. Jeremiah's greatest sorrow is that, because of the threat of war, he is told, "You shall not take a wife, nor shall you have sons or daughters. . . . For thus says the Lord concerning the sons and daughters who are born in this place, and concerning the mothers who bore them . . . : They shall die of deadly diseases. They shall not be lamented, nor shall they be buried; they shall be as dung on the surface of the ground. They shall perish by the sword and by famine, and their dead bodies shall be food for the birds of the air and for the beasts of the earth" (Jer. 16:1-4). Psalm 78:63 puts it more succinctly: "Fire devoured their young men, and their maidens had no marriage song."

Not content with denying that wars were holy, with affirming they were patently the result of sin, with grimly picturing their hideousness, the prophets developed quite a different theory of why Israel, "the smallest of all nations" (Deut. 7:7, NEB), had a place in the sun.

2

Not by Military Might

Old soldiers never die; they just keep on reciting tales of heroism and exploits of one's comrades that grow ever more glorious in the telling. Old Testament narratives recount military victories, but these are seldom referred to in the rest of Scripture. Nor does the Hebrew calendar contain any memory of men at war. It revolves about the seasons of the natural year (cf. Exod. 23:14–17), and contains no Fourth of July, no San Jacinto Day, no Bastille Day, no Red Sea Day, no Jericho Day, no Ai Day. Later Judaism added two other observances. The novella "Esther" tells of Purim, a secular carnival apparently derived from Babylonian sources. 1 Maccabees 4:52–56 relates how, after Antiochus had profaned the temple, a new altar was erected. At the dedication (John 10:22), "All the people worshiped and blessed Heaven, who had prospered them."

Foreign kings set up monuments to commemorate victories over foes. The monuments of the Old Testament do not mark the places where battles were fought; they do not show generals astride prancing steeds; they do not represent beaten enemies bowing in submission. In Israel, twelve stones mark the spot where the Ark of the Covenant, carried on the shoulders of the priests, safely crossed the Jordan (cf. Josh. 3:17–4:9). Commemorated, too, are Jacob's resting place the night he had a dream of heaven's proximity to earth (cf. Gen. 28:10–18) and the site where Jacob and his two-time father-in-law reconciled their differences (cf. Gen. 31:45, 52). A stone marked the spot where the Ark of the Covenant rested when it was returned by the Philistines (cf. 1 Sam. 6:18).

15

New Testament summaries of Old Testament history contain little recollection of armies or battles or conquest. Stephen, first martyr for the gospel, defended himself by recalling how all the Hebrew ages had been preparation for Messiah's coming (cf. Acts 7:2–53). His only hint of triumph over other nations is in connection with "the tent of witness," which "our fathers . . . brought . . . in with Joshua when they dispossessed the nations which God thrust out before our fathers" (vs. 44–45). The important thing is that "the tent of witness," focal point of worship, came in at the same time as Joshua, whose achievements go unmentioned. He did not even drive the Canaanites out, for God had gone before to clear the way!

The letter to the Hebrews, addressed to persecuted Christians of Jewish background, is concerned to demonstrate the superiority of Jesus to Moses, to angels, and to the Levitical priesthood. Its eleventh chapter vividly sets forth the accomplishments of those who have lived by "conviction of things not seen" (vs. 1). Its catalog of heroic deeds wrought by faith does not celebrate the triumphs of Joshua nor the conquest of the Land of Promise. Without mentioning the commander in chief, it says merely: "By faith the walls of Jericho fell down" (vs. 30).

Having got through Hebrew history without mentioning any military hero, the author of the letter, writing for those familiar with Hebrew lore, concludes (11:32): "And what more shall I say? For time would fail me to tell of Gideon, Barak, Samson, Jephthah, of David and Samuel and the prophets"—and leaves them at that, telling us nothing at all about them. It would be as if one should recount American history in terms of the Pilgrim Fathers, Roger Williams, the brothers Mather, Jonathan Edwards, and Phillips Brooks, and conclude: "Time would fail if I should tell of George Washington or Robert E. Lee or Douglas MacArthur."

Israel, the Chosen People

Historical events contributed to the demythologizing of military might. Israel's stance was viewed differently after the exile, when it lost its land to the Babylonians. The feeling of the nation boiled over into the bitterest and most shocking of all psalms: "O daughter of Babylon, you devastator! Happy shall he be who requites you with what you have done to us! Happy shall he be who takes your little ones and dashes them against the rock!" (Ps. 137:8f.). However, the defeat of their army and the loss of their homeland brought realization to Israel of what it truly meant to be Chosen People. Reinterpreting Israel's fundamental belief about itself, the prophets found new and deeper meaning.

The doctrine of the Chosen People did not mean that God had chosen Israel to lead the life of Reilly but, rather, that God had chosen them to be the bearers of his revelation. Isaiah of the Exile heard God say: "I have given you as a covenant to the people, a light to the nations, to open the eyes that are blind, to bring out the prisoners from the dungeon, from the prison those who sit in darkness. . . . I will give you as a light to the nations, that my salvation may reach to the end of the earth" (42:6–7; 49:6).

God always works through picked people. God picked the Greeks to give the world philosophy, the Italians to give it opera, the Hebrews to give it the secret of his redeeming love. Israel is the nation for others. A light does not shine for itself, but spends itself in giving illumination to the world. The prophet Amos (9:7) pointed out that God did not love Israel better than he loved others: "Are you not," God asks, "like the Ethiopians to me, O people of Israel?" If Israel is to be a light to those who sit in darkness, it does not mean that God has less love for those who are in darkness.

If Israel is to bring justice on earth, it does not mean that God cares less for those who suffer injustice. On the contrary, it is because God loves the whole world that he has chosen Israel to be the messenger of his love. Isaiah of the Exile sensed that this did not mean that Israel was exempt from the trials and tribulations faced by other nations. Rather Israel, if it is to be true to its mission, must assume the burdens of a common humanity. He therefore pictures Israel as humankind's Suffering Servant: "Surely he has borne our griefs and carried our sorrows; yet we esteemed him stricken, smitten of God, and afflicted. But he was wounded for our transgressions, he was bruised for our iniquities; upon him was the chastisement that made us whole, and with his stripes we are healed" (53:4f.).

Historians of a later time represent something of this as present from the beginning. Moses, wondering what might befall the disorganized mob he had led out of Egypt, asked for reassurance. God's promise was, "My presence will go with you" (Exod. 33:14). Eager still to be bolstered, Moses insisted, ". . . show me thy glory" (33:18). To that God's answer was, "I will make all my goodness pass before you" (33:19). Generations later, Nehemiah, giving thanks for God's guiding hand in his nation's history, rejoices in a well-furnished Land of Promise where his forebears "delighted themselves in thy great goodness" (9:25). It is impossible for Moses to gaze upon the face of God, and so find out all that God is. He is assured, however, that God's goodness will unfold before him and the pilgrim community he leads.

Every stratum of Old Testament literature acknowledges that everything Israel has is due, not to its own merit or achievement, but to the unmerited goodness of God. To that goodness, God's people attributed the way by which they had been led and the wonders they had witnessed. "Miracle" may be defined as God's use of his own law-abiding powers to work out, in ways unknown to us, his will for humankind. He who sees the end from the beginning does not have to read *Time* magazine or the "Week in Review" to find out what is going on in his world. God employs the powers at his command—the powers that keep the stars in their courses and bring about the rise and fall of nations—to work out his purpose of good.

God manifests himself in ways laid bare to those who have eyes to see. The Hebrews interpreted their experience in terms of the world about them. The blessing God promised to Noah, that never again would he wipe out all human life, had its reminder in every clear shining rainbow. That would be a sacramental sign not only for humankind but also for God: "When the bow is in the clouds, I will look upon it and remember the everlasting covenant" (Gen. 9:16).

Thinking of the unlikely way in which a nation of hod-carriers found itself encamped before Sinai, the historian imagines God saying to Moses, "You have seen . . . how I bore you on eagles' wings and brought you to myself" (Exod. 19:4). Slogging it out past the bitter waters of Marah, the waterless camp at Rephidim, and the hostility of the Amalekites was hardly riding high in the sky. Yet the wonder of escape from Egyptian slave-drivers to the Mountain of Revelation simply had to be the first Near Eastern airlift! So the Hebrews continued to interpret the goodness of God in terms of phenomena daily observed.

Isaiah (19:1) sees the Lord himself "riding on a swift cloud . . . and the idols of Egypt will tremble at his presence." God makes the clouds his chariot; he rides on the wings of the wind; he makes fire and flame his ministering servants (cf. Ps. 104:3). His way, thinks Nahum (1:3), "is in whirlwind and storm, and the clouds are the dust of his feet." Sinai was a volcanic mountain. Israel "came near and stood at the foot of the mountain, while the mountain burned with fire to the heart of heaven, wrapped in darkness, cloud, and gloom" (Deut. 4:11). There "the Lord spoke with you face to face . . . out of the midst of the fire" (Deut. 5:4). Fire has many modes: light, warmth, purification, punishment, retribution, destruction.

Mountains were ever after thought of as places where the divine goodness was manifest. Good news was proclaimed from mountaintops: "How beautiful upon the mountains are the feet of him who brings good tidings, who publishes peace" (Isa. 52:7; cf. Nah. 1:15). The mountains silently proclaim God's steadfast love (cf. Ps. 36:6; 76:4; Isa. 54:10). The prophet half expected the voice of the wooded height to be lifted up in praise to the Creator of all good: "Break forth into singing, O mountains, O forest and every tree in it!" (Isa. 44:23; cf. 49:13; 55:12; Ps. 114:4).

Vegetation itself was seen as evidence of the goodness of God: "The trees of the Lord are watered abundantly, the cedars of Lebanon which he planted. In them the birds build their nests, the stork has her home in the fir trees" (Ps. 104:16f.). Life as God intended it is to be lived out by the human family in appreciation of these manifestations of the goodness of God: "They shall sit every man under his vine and under his fig tree, and none shall make them afraid" (Mic. 4:4).

To people who thought like that, war could only be a disruption wrought by those who "fill the land with violence" and provoke the Eternal to anger (cf. Ezek. 8:17). Sirach's praise of famous men includes Joshua, the son of Nun, "mighty in war," who "waged the wars of the Lord. Was not the sun held back by his hand? And did not one day become as long as two?" (Ecclus. 46:1, 3f.). Canonical Scripture has no such praise; except for passing mention in 1 Kings 16:34, the name of Joshua does not appear in the Old Testament apart from the books Exodus to Judges, which recount the conquest of Canaan.

Hebrew summaries of the national epic do not boast of what forbears achieved through force of arms. Instead, they attribute everything to the goodness of God. Psalm 78 recapitulates what "our fathers have told us" about the nation's early history: "We will . . . tell to the coming generation the glorious deeds of the Lord, and his might, and the wonders which he has wrought" (vss. 3, 4). God's provision for the clans in the wilderness forms one of the themes. Study of desert flora and fauna leads to the conclusion that the biblical manna was "the liquid honeydew excretion of a number of cicadas, plant lice, and scale insects," which "speedily solidifies by rapid evaporation."[1]

Relating how the goodness of God made this appear at precisely the right time for the wilderness wanderers, the psalmist says that God "opened the doors of heaven; and he rained down upon them manna to eat" (78:23–24). Similarly with the quails that also appeared at the opportune moment: "He caused the east wind to blow . . . and by his power he led out the south wind; he rained flesh upon them like dust, winged birds like the sand of the seas" (78:26f.). The same wondrous provision is described more prosaically in Numbers 11:31: "And there went forth a wind from the Lord, and it brought quails from the sea, and let them fall beside the camp, about a day's journey on this side and a day's journey on the other side, . . . about two cubits deep on the face of the earth." As we know today, quails migrating from Africa to Europe in the spring pass over the Gulf of Aqaba region, and, often exhausted from the long over-water flight, are frequently forced by prevailing winds onto land along the way. They are still sold on the market for food.

Psalm 78 continues then with the settlement in Canaan. Verses 54f. say, "And he brought them to his holy land, . . . he drove out nations before them; he apportioned them for a possession and settled the tribes of Israel in their tents." No mention of Joshua and his forces; God did it by the exercise of his power. The Hebrews had their armies, but history taught them how right Samuel was in depicting the effect that reliance on kings and armies would have upon their society (cf. 1 Sam. 8:10ff.). Experience taught them the futility of trust in military equipment. This led another of their inspired poets to write, "Some boast of chariots, and some of horses; but we boast of the name of the Lord our God. They will collapse and fall; but we shall rise and stand upright" (Ps. 20:7f.).

Any one of several historical situations could have been in the author's mind. Some think the reference is to the Syrian invasion under Antiochus, whose policies met with such stubborn non-cooperation that oppressive cruelty proved powerless. At an earlier time, there had been an invasion by Sennacherib, King of Assyria, who came up against Judah, captured forty-six fortresses, and carried some 200,000 persons into captivity. Hezekiah tried a policy of appeasement. He sent rich presents: thirty talents of gold, three hundred talents of silver, precious stones, lovely maidens, and servants. He even stripped the gold from the temple doors and laid bare the royal treasury. When this did not suffice, he tried a military alliance with Egypt. Isaiah denounced this strategy: "Woe to those who go down to Egypt for help and rely on horses, who trust in chariots because they are many and in horsemen because they are very strong, but do not look to the Holy One of Israel or consult the Lord!" (31:1).

If trust were placed in Egypt, the prophet saw, that would be simply to exchange one tyranny for another. "Therefore shall the protection of Pharaoh turn to your shame, and the shelter in the shadow of Egypt to your humiliation" (Isa. 30:3). The invading king ridiculed the advice which the prophet offered: "Has any of the gods of the nations ever delivered his land out of the hand of the king of Assyria? Where are the gods of Hamath and Arpad . . . Sepharvaim, Hena, and Ivvah? . . . Who among all the gods of the countries have delivered their countries out of my hand, that the Lord should deliver Jerusalem out of my hand?" (2 Kings 18:33–35).

Hezekiah's prayer was, "Of a truth, O Lord, the kings of Assyria have laid waste the nations and their lands, . . . So now, O Lord our God, save us, I beseech thee, from his hand, that all the kingdoms of the earth may know that thou, O Lord, art God alone" (2 Kings 19:17–19). Isaiah (cf. 2 Kings 19:20) hears God say, "I will defend this city" (2 Kings 19:34). It seemed a forlorn hope; for Sennacherib, boasting of what he could do, was already thundering at the gates. Deliverance came in a way nobody could have foreseen: "And that night the angel of the Lord went forth, and slew a hundred and eighty-five thousand in the camp of the Assyrians; and when men arose early in the morning, behold, these were all dead bodies. Then Sennacherib . . . departed, and went home" (2 Kings 19:35f.), where he soon lost his life at the hands of his own sons.

Perhaps this rescue is enshrined, too, in Psalm 34:7: "The angel of the Lord encamps around those who fear him, and delivers them." Herodotus tells not of an angel but of natural forces used to effect this great deliverance.[2] The army of Sennacherib was routed because the strings of their bows and the thongs of their shields were devoured overnight by an army of field mice. Since rodents are known to migrate in time of plague, it may have been that cholera or some other disease carried by mice caused the death of Sennacherib's men. In any case, Hebrew king and prophet and people attributed this deliverance to the Lord: certain they were that their own strong right arms had nothing to do with it.

The deliverance from Egypt is the great and determining factor in Israel's history and remains the paradigm of God's dealing with his people. The New Testament interprets Jesus' death and resurrection in its terms. Luke 9:30f. tells how on the holy mountain Moses and Elijah, representing in their own persons the law and the prophets, "appeared in glory" and conversed with Jesus about "his departure, which he was to accomplish at Jerusalem." The word translated "departure" is *éxodon,* precisely the Septuagint term "exodus."

Preparing for his own "going out," Jesus arranged to eat the traditional Passover meal with his disciples (cf. Luke 22:7-13), and in so doing gave it a new significance: "I have earnestly desired to eat this passover with you before I suffer; for I tell you I shall not eat it until it is fulfilled in the kingdom of God" (Luke 22:15f.). Preparing for their "going out" from Egypt, each Hebrew family sacrificed a lamb, placing its blood upon "the two doorposts and the lintel" of their homes, so that "no plague shall fall upon you to destroy you, when I smite the land of Egypt" (Exod. 12:7, 13; Hebrews 11:28 has it: "so that the Destroyer of the first-born might not touch them").

As further preparation for departure, the Hebrews ate bread

hastily prepared. There was not time for leaven to do its work: "you shall eat it in haste" (Exod. 12:11). Paul uses this imagery to portray Jesus' own self-giving: "For Christ, our paschal lamb, has been sacrificed. Let us, therefore, celebrate the festival, not with the old leaven, the leaven of malice and evil, but with the unleavened bread of sincerity and truth" (1 Cor. 5:7f.).

Deliverance from Bondage

For Christians, as for Jews, exodus retains its symbolism as deliverance from bondage, whether to Egyptian taskmasters or to "sin which clings so closely" (Heb. 12:1). An often overlooked feature of the exodus is that the liberation from Egyptian bondage was accomplished without the use of violence on the part of those liberated. Moses had "refused to be called the son of Pharaoh's daughter, choosing rather to share ill-treatment with the people of God than to enjoy the fleeting pleasures of sin" (Heb. 11:24f.). Leaving the sheltered life of the Pharaoh's court—where, not incidentally, he had acquired the best education then to be had—he quickly became aware of the hardships his people were suffering and the indignities to which they were subjected.

Moses' first impulse was to launch a guerrilla campaign. Seeing an Egyptian beating a Hebrew, "He looked this way and that, and seeing no one he killed the Egyptian and hid him in the sand" (Exod. 2:11–12). Shortly thereafter when Pharaoh sought to put an end to him and his incipient revolt, Moses took refuge in the land of Midian, where, in a vision at the bush that burned but was not consumed, he was commissioned to lead a different kind of freedom movement: "I will send you to Pharaoh that you may bring forth my people . . . out of Egypt" (Exod. 3:10).

This act of deliverance was accomplished without the need for Hebrews to kill a single Egyptian. God's power at work in the natural world accomplished what was needed. A succession of plagues softened up the resistance. When "a strong east wind" (Exod. 14:21) opened a path through the Sea of Reeds, or Red Sea, the Hebrews went through on dry land, "but the Egyptians, when they attempted to do the same, were drowned" (Heb. 11:29). Miriam's song celebrates this victory accomplished by a power not their own: "Sing to the Lord, for he has triumped gloriously; the horse and his rider he has thrown into the sea" (Exod. 15:21; a more elaborate description of the drowning is in Exod. 15:4–12).

The same would be true with the victory at Jericho. Song and story tell how Joshua "fought the battle of Jericho." The Hexateuch narrative concludes: "Then they utterly destroyed all in the city, both men and women, young and old, oxen, sheep, and asses, with the edge of the sword" (Josh. 6:21). There was thus carried out the *herem*, "an irrevocable alienation from common use, perhaps originally an act of renunciation by the warrior,"[3] who refused plunder or personal profit from an operation designed to aid in obliterating false religion.

The historian tells, however, that it was not by violence that the city of Jericho came into their possession: this was the end product of purely psychological warfare. For six successive days, Joshua and his men marched silently around the walled city, the Lord himself moving with them, his presence symbolized in the ark carried by the priests. On the seventh day the procession moved around the city not once but seven times; the priests blew "the seven trumpets of rams' horns" (Josh. 6:13). The people "raised a great shout, and the wall fell down flat, so that the people went up into the city, every man straight before him, and they took the city" (Josh. 6:20).

Archaeology has disclosed that it was not the trumpet blasts or the shouts of the people but God's power at work in the natural world that leveled the walls. Excavations indicate "a four- or five-acre city surrounded by a double wall. The city was destroyed in a great conflagration apparently assisted by an earthquake";[4] "the outer wall fell mostly outward down the hill, while the stronger inner wall collapsed into the space between the two walls."[5]

The triumph at Jericho was decisive for the occupation of the Land of Promise, and it was accomplished by the mysterious natural forces under control of the Lord of heaven and earth who "thunders wondrously with his voice; he does great things which we cannot comprehend. . . . He loads the thick cloud with moisture; the clouds scatter his lightning. They turn round and round by his guidance, to accomplish all that he commands them on the face of the habitable world. Whether for correction, or for his land, or for love, he causes it to happen" (Job 37:5, 11–13).

Following the occupation of Jericho, there were to be many other skirmishes and several successive waves of immigrants before the Land of Promise could be thought of as the Hebrew homeland. Other tribes had to be displaced: Amorites, Perizzites, Canaanites, Hittites, Girgashites, Hivites, Jebusites (cf. Josh. 24:11), but the occupiers were never allowed to think that by their own prowess all this was accomplished: "I sent the hornet before you"—the hornet was a symbol of Pharaoh—"which drove them out before you, . . . it was not by your sword or by your bow. I gave you a land on which you had not labored, and cities which you had not built, and you dwell therein; you eat the fruit of vineyards and oliveyards which you did not plant" (Josh. 24: 12–13).

The victory of Deborah and Barak over the army of Sisera was the culmination of the Hebrew settlement of the Land of Promise. Sisera, military leader for a coalition of Canaanite kings, came against the Hebrews with "nine hundred chariots of iron" (Judg. 4:3). Two accounts of the battle survive: a prose version in Judges 4:1–22, and a poetic one in 5:19–31. Poetry precedes prose in a people's history, and the Song of Deborah, composed nearer the time of the event it describes, appears to be more original as well as more colorful than the later prose narrative.

Both accounts picture the ignominious end of Sisera, the mighty warrior, commander of troops and chariots, who lost his life at the hands of a woman (cf. Judg. 4:17–21; 5:24–27). The poem reaches its climax in a highly imaginative portrayal of Sisera's mother sitting at the window and wondering why her soldier son is so long in returning. She and her princesses conclude that the general has been delayed by a mopping-up operation:

Are they not finding and dividing the spoil?—
A maiden or two for every man;
spoil of dyed stuffs for Sisera,
spoil of dyed stuffs embroidered,
two pieces of dyed work embroidered for my neck as spoil?
[Judges 5:30]

The narrative relates prosaically that Sisera left his chariot and fled, "and all the army of Sisera fell by the edge of the sword; not a man was left" (Judg. 4:15f.). The poetic version puts it very differently, attributing the victory not to the prowess of Barak and his troops but to natural powers ordered for their advantage. A sudden downpour changed the brook Kishon into a raging torrent in which the bogged-down charioteers were drowned as they tried to squeeze through the narrow valley at the western end of the Plain of Esdraelon. There were heavenly allies, too:

> From heaven fought the stars,
>   from their courses they fought against Sisera.
> The torrent Kishon swept them away,
>   the onrushing torrent, the torrent Kishon
>   [Judges 5:20f.].

One of David's most celebrated victories was won without the usual military accoutrement. As a youth, setting out to battle the Philistine challenger, he buckled on his armor: huge helmet and coat-of-mail. Then he fastened on his sword—and found himself so swathed in military gear that he was immobilized. Thereupon he threw off the armor and chose five smooth stones from the brook. These proved four too many, for with a single pebble from his slingshot he brought down the giant (cf. 1 Sam. 17:39–49). This, says the historian (vs. 47), was in order "that all this assembly may know that the Lord saves not with sword and spear."

The horse was the MX missile of the time, deployed by the great empires of the day. Job 39:19–25 describes the war-horse, which "smells the battle from afar" (vs. 25) and champs at the bit: "he cannot stand still at the sound of the trumpet." The Hebrews were reluctant, however, to adopt this big-power weapon. Moses warned that a subsequent ruler "must not multiply horses for himself" (Deut. 17:16). Samuel feared that if Israel chose a king he would come to depend for his defense upon this symbol of luxury and physical power (1 Sam. 8:11–12).

Solomon was well provided with this battle force. His cavalry was famous; and his neatly arranged stables at Megiddo have been unearthed. Yet Psalm 33:16f. points out the limitations of such high-spirited, high-powered steeds: "A king is not saved by his great army; a warrior is not delivered by his great strength, the war horse is a vain hope for victory, and by its great might it cannot save." The Rabshakeh, an official of the Assyrian Empire, taunted King Hezekiah: "I will give you two thousand horses, if you are able on your part to set riders upon them" (2 Kings 18:23). Two thousand riderless horses would be a gift unmanageable! Worse than useless, they would create havoc in a stampede. Nahum 3:3 pictures what happens to those who trust in horses: "Horsemen charging, flashing sword and glittering spear, hosts of slain, heaps of corpses, dead bodies without end—they stumble over the bodies."

The prophetic judgment upon military power is summed up in the word of the Lord which came through the prophet Zechariah to King Zerubbabel: "Not by might, nor by power, but by my Spirit, says the Lord of hosts" (Zech. 4:6).

The Meaning of the Goodness of God

Reliance upon the goodness of God enables human beings and nations to triumph over obstacles. God's goodness, however, has its sterner side. Love cannot abide that which would destroy love. The converse of Holy Love is Holy Wrath. This does not refer to personal vindictiveness but to God's settled opposition to sin and evil. The letter to the Hebrews, written at a time of international upheaval, pictures God as shaking "not only the earth but also the heaven" (12:26). This should cause neither surprise nor consternation: things are being shaken up "in order that what cannot be shaken may remain" (12:27). The believer's reaction therefore should be: ". . . let us be grateful for receiving a kingdom that cannot be shaken, and thus let us offer to God acceptable worship, with reverence and awe; for our God is a consuming fire" (12:28f.).

Fire and wrath as instruments of divine justice are not to be invoked by humankind. When Jesus and his disciples were refused hospitality in one community, James and John put the question squarely: " 'Lord, do you want us to bid fire come down from heaven and consume them?' But he turned and rebuked them. And they went on to another village" (Luke 9:54f.). Some manuscripts here insert words that explain Jesus' rebuke: "You do not know what manner of spirit you are of; for the Son of man came not to destroy men's lives but to save them."

Human beings do not need to call down fire from heaven, increase the fire power of their weapons, or conjure up atomic fire, for God is still in control: ". . . will not God vindicate his elect, who cry to him day and night? Will he delay long over them? I tell you, he will vindicate them speedily" (Luke 18:7f.). War is sometimes urged upon us on the ground that, in order to vindicate the right, we must destroy the evil. A fundamentalist Christian once said he believed it was his duty to wipe out Germans in World War I because German scholarship had led people to doubt the Bible.

Paul, who had learned from Jesus that humankind must not play God, put it this way: "Beloved, never avenge yourselves, but leave it to the wrath of God; for it is written, 'Vengeance is mine, I will repay, says the Lord.' No, 'if your enemy is hungry, feed him; if he is thirsty, give him drink; for by so doing you will heap burning coals upon his head.' Do not be overcome by evil, but overcome evil with good" (Rom. 12:19–21).

Ancient sculptures show Egyptian, Assyrian, and Persian kings proudly riding in horse-drawn chariots. When Jesus entered Jerusalem, there was fulfilled a different ideal of human relationships: "Behold, your king is coming to you, humble, and mounted . . . on a colt, the foal of an ass" (Matt. 21:5, quoting Zech. 9:9).

3

Prophet to the Nations

Prophets never peddled purely private oracles. From the out-set, Jeremiah is told, "I appointed you a prophet to the nations" (1:5). Amos, pronouncing God's judgment upon Middle Eastern life in the eighth century B.C., specifies the transgressions not only of his own nation, Israel and Judah, but also of Edom, Moab, and Ammon. Some of Ezekiel's most vivid and powerful passages are addressed to Tyre, Sidon, and Philistia. Micah begins his public ministry with the words, "Attend, all nations, listen O earth and all on earth. The Eternal has a warning for you" (1:2, M).

In the Prophetic Tradition

Jesus' first sermon in his home town unmistakably identified him with this tradition. The synagogue service had two lessons for each day. The one from the law was fixed in a kind of lectionary. The other, from the prophets, was of the reader's choosing. Addressing those who had known him from boyhood, Jesus "found the place where it was written, 'The Spirit of the Lord is upon me, because he has anointed me to preach good news to the poor. He has sent me to proclaim release to the captives and recovering of sight to the blind, to set at liberty those who are oppressed, to proclaim the acceptable year of the Lord' " (Luke 4:17-19, quoting Isa. 61:1f.).

What then? Luke makes a point of saying, "And he closed the book." He closed the book before reading the next line, which is "and the day of vengeance of our God." For Jesus this is a part of

29

the old order that has dropped out. In his use of the Old Testament, Jesus always practiced what George Adam Smith called "a great discrimination." The passage that Jesus did read outlines his program (cf. Luke 7:20f.). It is a kind of précis of all that he was to do. He came to announce good news to the poor. The word here used for "poor" suggests not genteel poverty but abject poverty: the poorest of the poor.

"To proclaim release to the captives": the word here describes those taken in war, those who fall into the enemy's hands at the point of a spear. "Recovering of sight to the blind": that is, captives in exile, some of whom had been blinded by their captors, others who had lost their sight through long confinement in a dungeon. "To set at liberty those who are oppressed": the word means broken in pieces, shattered, crushed by calamity, those crushed in spirit and shattered in fortune by war.

From all these concomitants of military action Jesus came to set us free. The original reference in Isaiah is to those who suffered these afflictions at the hands of the Babylonians. Ultimately they were liberated and allowed to return to the much loved homeland (cf. Ps. 137:1–6). For all its suffering, the exile was the most creative epoch in Hebrew history. "Good news" and "proclaim" are Greek concepts used in the Septuagint rendering of the Isaiah passage for the first time in the sense that has become dear to the church. Preaching came to take its place side by side with sacramental worship in the life of the nation. The synagogue pulpit became as much the center of Israel's life as the temple altar once had been.

Jesus' sermon in Nazareth sets forth his intent in coming into the world. Everything he did was in fulfillment of it. That was his program. It must be the program, too, of his church. He was "sent," appointed, consecrated to proclaim good news to the poor and the oppressed. That must be the program of his church. Prophets were sent to their time; Jesus was sent to his time; the church is sent to its time. The climactic words of John's Gospel are, "As the Father has sent me, even so I send you" (20:21).

Prophets addressed themselves both to individuals and to nations. The church has too often forgotten that Jesus did this, too. It is certain that what Jesus said to his disciples did not cause him to be crucified. He was not crucified for saying, "Consider the lilies of the field" or "In my Father's house are many rooms," nor even for "Love one another" or "Do unto others as you would that they should do to you." Was he crucified because "he went about doing good?" Certainly not! He was crucified because two nations—one great, one small: Rome and Israel—were scandalized by his vision of a kingdom outstripping anything of which either of them had dreamed.

The Ministry of Jesus

Jesus lived all his life in an occupied country. The Roman armies of occupation regarded his little land, his people, and himself with contempt. When he says, "if anyone forces you to go one mile, go with him two miles" (Matt. 5:41), he has in mind the overriding and insulting demands of the invaders. A Roman soldier could commandeer a civilian, any civilian, to carry his pack—and Jesus counsels doing more than is required, killing with kindness. A mile south of Megiddo there is a village still called El-Jejjun, from "Legion," the site of a Roman army encampment, just as those far-away British cities—Lancaster, Rochester, Winchester—still bear the marks of their origin as *castra,* the Roman word for army camp.

When Jesus, outside the city of Gerasa, found a demon-possessed man living among the caves used for tombs and cutting his unshod feet on the sharp stones of the hillside, Jesus said to him, "What is your name?"—that is to say, "What did your mother call you? How were you known in the family? Who were you before this happened to you?" The answer Jesus received was different from what he might have expected: "My name is Legion" (Mark 5:9). Feeling as he did, possessed by a thousand demons, the poor man could think only of the Roman army. Had he been driven crazy by the clank, clank of the hobnailed boots marching up and down the land, troops forcing him to carry loads too heavy for him, expecting his mother to feed them, demanding that his father turn over a third of his income?

At the outset of his ministry, Jesus faced the question of how best to deal with a situation involving his people in so much hardship and tension. Among his compatriots were freedom fighters who were urging violent opposition to Rome. If they only had

Jesus at their head to command their small armies, they might win a momentary victory: "the devil took him to a very high mountain, and showed him all the kingdoms of the world and the glory of them" (Matt. 4:8). Early commentators noted that there is no mountain—not even a peak in Lebanon—from which one can see all the kingdoms of the world.

Plainly, this is a symbolic experience. Luke (4:5–8) indeed says that "the devil . . . showed him all the kingdoms of the world in a moment of time, and said to him, 'To you I will give all this authority and their glory. . . if you . . . will worship me.' " That would have been to assume imperial power, a temptation Jesus promptly rejected: "It is written, 'You shall worship the Lord your God, and him only shall you serve.' " It is widely assumed that Jesus, having rejected the possibility of seizing imperial rule over subject people, at once and forever turned his back upon the nations.

That is not true, and it is impossible to imagine why it has been so long taken for granted. Jesus' ministry brought encounter with a surprising variety of outsiders: a woman of Syrophoenicia, a demoniac in Transjordan, a company of Greeks who sought him out in the temple courts at Jerusalem. His teaching makes reference to historical events involving Israel's relationships with other nations. He recalls Lot's unhappy experience on the day when Lot left Sodom and "fire and brimstone rained from heaven and destroyed them all" (Luke 17:29). He reminds his hearers, too, that in the day of judgment the Son of man will be to his generation as Jonah was to the Ninevites.

One with sympathies like that could not abide the negations with which his orthodox compatriots insulated themselves: not eating with foreigners, not talking to Samaritans, not wanting to be seen in the company of "sinners." The idea of the Chosen People, narrowly interpreted as most-favored-nation treatment for Jews, is completely discarded in Jesus' descriptions of the inclusiveness of his kingdom. (Carl Sandburg once said that the ugliest term in the English language is the word "exclusive.") Jesus was careless of the company he kept. He was not ashamed to be seen with tax collectors, winos, gluttons, or prostitutes. This made him unacceptable to those among his own people who, drawing around them a cloak of respectability, regarded themselves as "holier than thou."

Due to an ancient falling-out, closely related Jews and Samaritans had little use for each other and no familiar dealings. Jesus appears to have gone out of his way to smash this taboo. Where other Galileans would have avoided Samaria on a journey to the south, he went straight through, conversed freely with a Samaritan woman he encountered at a public watering-place, made distinctive revelation of God to her ("God is Spirit . . . neither on this mountain nor in Jerusalem will you worship" John 4:24, 21), went to her home village and received recognition there not elsewhere accorded him ("this is indeed the Savior of the world," John 4:42). No citizen of Judah had ever said a thing like that!

Luke has two other instances in which Jesus not only shows no enmity to Samaritans but praises them. When a Jew falls among thieves who strip him and beat him and leave him for dead, his rescuer is not a priest or a Levite, both of whom were hurrying away to keep appointments at the temple, but a Samaritan. Lepers were outcasts and Jesus encountered ten of them huddled together for mutual support and encouragement. Misery knows no distinction of race or class, and this group was ethnically mixed. Jesus healed them all. Only one ever came back to give thanks, "Now he was a Samaritan" (Luke 17:16). The Fourth Gospel makes it clear that Jesus' own people so resented all this that they sneeringly referred to him as a demon-possessed Samaritan (cf. John 8:48).

As if quiet example were not enough, Jesus made it explicit to his fellow Hebrews that God's favor was not exclusively theirs (Matt. 8:11f.): "I tell you, many will come from east and west [Luke 13:29 adds "and from north and south"] and sit at table with Abraham, Isaac, and Jacob, . . . while the sons of the kingdom will be thrown into outer darkness; there men will weep and gnash their teeth." To the pious who thought that wearing proper phylacteries and making long prayers would save them, Jesus said: "the tax collectors and the harlots go into the kingdom of God before you" (Matt. 21:31).

At the day of judgment, Ninevites would be in a better position than Hebrews, for Ninevites repented when they had a chance (cf.

Luke 11:32). Jesus reminded them, too, of the Queen of Sheba (the modern Yemen in the southwestern part of the Arabian peninsula), who made a long journey to wonder at the wisdom of King Solomon, and who was a rebuke to Jesus' contemporaries because she knew a good thing when she saw it. Jesus' hearers did not have to make a long journey: the kingdom of God had been opened to them, and they did not have the wit to recognize it.

It was not long before Jesus' own community, tired of being disturbed by him, was plotting his death on the charges of blasphemy, breaking the Sabbath, and of cooperating with Beelzebul to make people think he was a wonder-worker. What really repelled them was his insistence that they were no better than any other of the men and women in God's creation. The Hebrews rejected Jesus because he told them that they had forfeited the kingdom. They had indeed carried out the minutiae of the law, but had little concern for the qualities of character that make a difference: ". . . you tithe mint and rue and every herb, and neglect justice and the love of God" (Luke 11:42). Matthew 23:23 has it: "you tithe mint and dill and cummin, and have neglected the weightier matters of the law, justice and mercy and faith." The symbol of Israel on Maccabean coins was the fig tree. Jesus pictured Israel as a fig tree, which made a show of fruit but had none. The Gospels report this as an acted parable, describing a fig tree that Jesus cursed as "withered away to its roots" (Mark 11:20).

Local political leadership in Palestine was subservient to the Romans. From 37 B.C. to A.D. 70 the Herod dynasty was in power. Jesus appears to have engaged in a kind of running battle with the Herods. It was Herod the Great who had made the infant Jesus a displaced person. Herod Antipas was the tetrarch who, fearing that the popularity of John the Baptizer might lead to a political uprising, had the prophet beheaded. News of John's death indicated to Jesus the need for caution, and "he withdrew from there in a boat to a lonely place"; already his popularity was so great that he could not find seclusion, for "the crowds followed him on foot from the towns" (Matt. 14:13).

This further disturbed Antipas, whose troubled conscience led him to think: "John the baptizer has been raised from the dead; that is why these powers are at work" (Mark 6:14). Jesus thereupon withdrew for a time to Tyre and Sidon (cf. Mark 7:24), thus bringing him once more into a foreign land. Tyre and Sidon were famed cities of the Phoenicians, whose ships plied all seas; whose merchantmen trafficked in goods from everywhere (cf. Ezek. chaps. 27–28); whose adventurers established colonies in Spain and North Africa. The Gospels do not record the reception Jesus received there, but the warmth of it is suggested when he reproaches his own Galilean communities: "Woe to you, Chorazin! woe to you, Beth-saida! for if the mighty works done in you had been done in Tyre and Sidon, they would have repented long ago" (Luke 10:13).

From there, Jesus went on to the Greek cities of the Decapolis, beyond the Jordan (cf. Mark 7:31). Soon his message included a warning against the influence of Antipas: "beware of the leaven of the Pharisees and the leaven of Herod" (Mark 8:15). Later in the ministry—the data are so scarce that we cannot precisely trace the chronology—some kindly disposed Pharisees came to Jesus to say, "Get away from here, for Herod wants to kill you" (Luke 13:31). Now confidently approaching the end, Jesus replied, "Go and tell that fox, 'Behold, I cast out demons and perform cures today and tomorrow, and the third day I finish my course. Nevertheless I must go on my way today and tomorrow and the day following; for it cannot be that a prophet should perish away from Jerusalem' " (Luke 13:32f.).

The fox in our folklore is the symbol of craftiness: "as sly as a fox," we say. In rabbinical thought, however, the fox typified an utter good-for-nothing. Here is Jesus' boldly expressed judgment upon the ruler of his province. One of Jesus' parables, that of the Pounds (cf. Luke 19:12ff.) actually holds the Herod family up to ridicule. It tells how "a nobleman went into a far country to receive kingly power and then return" (vs. 12). Meanwhile he entrusted to his servants various sums of money: when he comes back, there will be a reckoning. While he was absent, his unhappy subjects sent an embassy after him, saying, "We do not want this man to reign over us" (vs. 14).

This could have been a story taken from the evening news. Upon the death of Herod the Great, a codicil of his will named Archelaus his principal successor. The claim was disputed by Antipas and Philip. The brothers appealed to Rome to settle the squabble. Meantime, rebellion had broken out back home, and a delegation arrived in Rome, petitioning Augustus to give the throne to none of the sons of Herod, and let the Jews live entirely by their own law.

Jesus versus Pilate

Jesus was equally bold in making known what he thought of the Roman authorities. For those who had eyes to see and ears to hear, he let it be known what opinion he held regarding Pilate and the empire whose minion he was. The Roman governor was concerned for his own position. As colonial administrator, Pilate already had demerits marked against him. It was Rome's policy to interfere as little as possible with local customs, particularly local religious rites and observances. Official policy called for deference to the Hebrew position on the use of images. In consideration of this strongly held predilection against their use, the Romans had gone to the length of removing from their military standards the figure of the emperor. Pilate, however, considering that this was unworthy of somebody who wanted to be Number One, had ordered the banners bearing the figure of the emperor to be carried into Jerusalem.

"Pilate," notes Josephus,[1] "was the first who brought these images" among citizens whose law "forbade the very making of images." When Judean delegations petitioned Pilate to remove these offending emblems, "he would not grant their request." When they persisted, he consented to another meeting, this one on a judgment seat so arranged as to conceal "the army that lay ready to oppress them; and when the Jews petitioned him again, he gave a signal to the soldiers" to attack. But the protesting citizens offered a novel form of nonviolent resistance: they "threw themselves on the ground, and laid their necks bare, and said they would take their death very willingly, rather than that the wisdom of their laws should be transgressed."

Thereupon Pilate, "deeply affected with their firm resolution to keep their laws inviolable . . . commanded the images to be carried back from Jerusalem " to the military headquarters at Caesarea. Antagonism, however, continued to develop. Pilate, says Josephus,[2] built an aqueduct bringing water to Jerusalem from a distance of some twenty-five miles. He paid for this with money that he took from the temple treasury. Naturally "the Jews were not pleased with what had been done about this water; and many ten thousands of the people got together and made a clamor against him, and insisted that he should leave off that design. Some of them also used reproaches and abused the man, as crowds of such people usually do."

Pilate then worked out another stratagem. He dressed his soldiers in civilian garb, so that they could not easily be distinguished from ordinary citizens. The disguised troops, with daggers under their garments, were deployed so as to surround the protesting throng. He then ordered the Jews to disperse. When they refused, he gave the signal for an attack. "Since the people were unarmed, and were caught by men prepared for what they were about, there were a great number of them slain by this means, and others of them ran away wounded."

Within the Gospels there is evidence that Pilate took advantage of Jewish religious festivals to massacre recalcitrant subjects. Luke 13:1 relates that a report was brought to Jesus concerning "Galileans whose blood Pilate had mingled with their sacrifices." It is not clear whether those who brought this report to Jesus were hoping it would lead him to open revolt, or whether they were merely looking for some expression of indignation that could be carried to Pilate as evidence of sedition. This leads Jesus to refer to "those eighteen, upon whom the tower in Siloam fell" (Luke 13:4). The tower of Siloam was a fortification near an important spring and reservoir. This may have something to do with a demonstration against Pilate's aqueduct, built with temple funds. Jesus does not here deal with the question of innocent suffering, but regards both catastrophes as solemn warnings: "unless you repent you will all likewise perish" (Luke 13:3).

Both incidents, briefly related as they are, do suggest the constant turmoil that marked the procuratorship of Pilate, who no doubt defended all these actions as necessary to the national security. Philo[3] tells of another circumstance in Pilate's administration, when Pilate, through "lack of consideration for the religious scruples of the Jews," was threatened by them with an appeal to Rome. Philo records Agrippa as saying that this exasperated Pilate "to the greatest degree, as he feared they might go on an embassy to the Emperor, and might impeach him with respect to other particulars of his government—his corruptions, his acts of insolence, his rapine, and his habits of insulting people, his cruelty, and his continual murder of people untried and uncondemned, and his never-ending and most grievous inhumanity."

Jesus' carefully chosen vocabulary further reveals his own opinion of the government under which he was condemned to live. When Rome began to conquer outlying territories and force them into a confederacy, it sought to soften the blow by calling its neighboring peoples not subjects but "allies and friends." Certain persons in other provinces, cherished for whatever reason by the emperor, received the title "Friend," a term synonymous with ally, comrade, courtier. The Judeans said to Pilate, "If you release this man, you are not Caesar's friend" (John 19:12). Jesus did not fail to point out that he had a different idea of friendship: "You are my friends if you do what I command you. . . . I have called you friends, for all that I have heard from my Father I have made known to you" (John 15:14f.).

For Jesus, all the world was a parable, and reference to other than human creatures could convey deep meaning to the discerning. Appropriately enough, the wolf was sacred to Mars, as a wolf had nourished Romulus, legendary founder and first king of Rome. Romulus and Remus were reputedly the twin sons of Rhea Silvia, by the god of war. Ordered to be drowned, the boys were miraculously saved, and suckled by a wolf. The Romans had proverbs about wolves: *lupus in fabula*—talk of a wolf and he appears. It was believed that a man seen by a wolf before he saw the wolf lost his speech. *Ambigui* was a term applied to men in the form of wolves. Was it the presence in his country of so many men trained and nourished by the Martian wolves that led Jesus to say to his friends, "Behold, I send you out as sheep in the midst of wolves" (Matt. 10:16)?

Matthew 24:28 and Luke 17:37 report a saying of Jesus' taken from an apocalyptic context. In picturesque imagery the apocalyptic writers picture God's expected judgment upon the world. Zephaniah, one of the earliest writers in this genre, delineates the doom of Nineveh, "the teeming city that sat so secure, that thought herself supreme, the only power!" (2:15, M). All now is changed, for "bitterns and pelicans rest on her pillars, owls hoot in her windows, ravens on her doorsteps" (2:14, M). When Jesus speaks in this idiom words that some consider to describe the impending end of the age, he may very well have had in mind the imminent destruction of Jerusalem by the Romans.

When asked concerning some of his imagery, "Where, Lord?" he answers, "Where the body is, there the eagles will be gathered together" (Luke 17:37). This is part of a passage in which Jesus envisages a fate comparable to that of Sodom and Gomorrah. One commentator thinks it may refer to "the rush of avenging forces wherever the life of a nation has fallen into dissolution and decay." The particular imagery Jesus uses, however, may have been suggested by the presence of the Roman legions: not bitterns nor pelicans nor hoot owls, but eagles. The Roman eagle was the imperial ensign. The introduction of that into Jerusalem, like the introduction of the emperor's image, was a cause of insurrection. "Where the body is, there the eagles will be." Does this picture the eagerness of the military always to be in on the kill? How far do martial men—the men of Mars—still suck the blood of humanity?

When at last Jesus, arrived in Jerusalem, is hailed before Pilate, the Roman procurator, hearing that the suspect was a Galilean and that the tetrarch of Galilee was in town that day, remanded Jesus to Herod, who pretended to be "very glad, for he had long desired to see him, because he had heard about him, and he was hoping to see some sign done by him" (Luke 23:8). When Jesus, knowing that Herod had no authority in Jerusalem, refused to answer the questions put to him, Herod "treated him with contempt and mocked him; then, arraying him in gorgeous apparel, he sent him back to Pilate. And Herod and Pilate became friends with each other that very day, for before this they had been at enmity" (Luke 23:11f.). Did ever friendship originate in such infamy?

By sending Jesus to Antipas, Pilate had hoped to place the onus upon the Jews, and the friendship thus formed perfectly exemplifies the combination of unholy forces that crucified Jesus. He would not allow himself to be the captive of any earthly monarch, whether a petty underling in Galilee or a procurator of the Roman empire. This is dramatized also in the references to Caesar in the Gospels. At the trial before Pilate, the accusation is: "We found this man perverting our nation, and forbidding us to give tribute to Caesar, and saying that he himself is Christ a king" (Luke 23:2). It was thought that such charges were best calculated to make him objectionable to Caesar's representative.

The only "perverting our nation" that Jesus ever did was to call it back to its high sense of mission, not as superior to others, but as chosen of God to be "a light to the nations." Nor had Jesus forbidden his fellow Palestinians to "give tribute to Caesar." As an inhabitant of the empire, he did not refuse to pay taxes, but rather used tax-collecting time to illustrate the essential nature of his universal kingdom, in contrast with that of Caesar's limited sovereignty. Sometimes a "truth squad" would accompany Jesus, seeking to "entrap him in his talk" (Mark 12:13; Matt. 22:46).

A delegation of Herodians—who enjoyed putting down small-town teachers who had made it to the big city—asked him, "Is it lawful to pay taxes to Caesar or not?" It was a loaded question. If he answered "Certainly!" he would alienate that considerable part of the population who resented not only the taxation exacted by Rome but also the repulsive characters who collected it. If he said "No!" that would appear to involve him in rebellion against the established order. In reply, he asked for a coin of the realm, in which the tax had to be paid. Noting that it bore "the likeness and inscription" of Caesar, he said, "Render to Caesar the things that are Caesar's." Reminding them that as human beings they bore "the likeness and inscription" of the divine Maker, he added, "and to God the things that are God's" (Mark 12:16–17). Honorable government has a right to collect the revenue that sustains the public weal, but not the right to tyrannize over men and women, who bear upon them the mark of divine origin.

If the charges advanced by the Palestinians had no substance, Pilate had his own reasons for desiring Jesus out of the way. We have seen the subtle ways in which Jesus put down Pilate and all who lorded it over their fellows. Jesus' appearance before Pilate points the contrast between the two men. Even to the casual observer, the outward appearance must have been strikingly different. Pilate, representative of Roman Imperium, was decked out in all the trappings of empire: a gorgeous uniform; a sword clanking heavily at his side; a bodyguard discreetly keeping watch; a multitude of attendants hovering around to care for every real and imagined need. Before him stood Jesus, the herald of God's kingdom. He wore a simple tunic such as any peasant might wear: woven all in one piece, no doubt by someone who loved him dearly. He had no sword or badge of might. He was unattended—even his friends kept at a respectful distance. "We are made to feel," as one has said, "the contrast between the calm, commanding figure of this King of Truth, and his flurried Roman judge, dressed in his little brief authority, but with no inner authority of soul."

The Gospels more than once mention Pilate's judgment seat. Matthew 27:19 reports that it was "while he was sitting on the judgment seat" that his wife sent to him her message of warning. John 19:13 notes that at one point during the trial of Jesus, Pilate "brought Jesus out and sat down on the judgment seat at a place called The Pavement." From there he would pronounce the judgment of empire upon one charged with sedition. The Fourth Gospel indicates that Jesus had a different idea of judgment: "And this is the judgment, that the light has come into the world, and men loved darkness rather than light, because their deeds were evil" (John 3:19).

The Kingdom of Truth

Jesus and Pilate did not speak the same language. Jesus' kingdom is the kingdom of Truth. Given a chance to speak in his own defense, Jesus affirms: "For this I have come into the world, to bear witness to the truth. Every one who is of the truth hears my voice" (John 18:37). Truth is correspondence of our ideas with reality. The kingdom of Truth has no frontiers, for all whose hearts and minds are open to the truth are drawn to him who said, "I am the way, and the truth, and the life" (John 14:6). The kingdom of Truth is not just for Jews; it would have room for Pilate, who heartily despised the Jews. To the declaration of Jesus there comes the half-skeptical, half-scornful, perhaps half-jesting reply of Pilate, made familiar to English readers by Bacon's famous essay: " 'What is truth?' said jesting Pilate, and would not stay for an answer."

Truth is one. Jesus prays for his people "that they may be one, even [Father] as we are one" (John 17:11). This is the direct opposite of the principle upon which Rome had built its empire: *divide et impera*—divide and rule! No rights of *connubium* or *commer-cium* were permitted to exist between or among the colonies. In keeping the dependencies separated, the intention was to prevent any coalition that might imperil the imperial power. The issue now is fully joined. Two nations are conspiring against Jesus. They find a way, they think, to get rid of him.

Will Rogers observed that humankind has undoubtedly made progress: each new war finds people killing each other with more effective weapons. Crucifixion was a refinement of torture not practiced by the Hebrews but official in the Roman world. Antici-pating that, under the circumstances, a cross might await him at journey's end, Jesus said, "I, when I am lifted up from the earth, will draw all men to myself" (John 12:32). Lest the point be missed, the Gospel writer adds (vs. 33), "He said this to show by what death he was to die." Hebrew and Roman conspired to elevate Jesus by means of two crossed beams and four nails.

Both Hebrew and Greek inadvertently recognized the universal drawing power of "that strange man upon his cross." Caiaphas, high priest that year in Jerusalem, said to his circle of advisers, who were uneasy about what might happen to their state if Jesus should be let loose in the world, ". . . it is expedient that one man should die for the people, and that the whole nation should not perish" (John 11:50). "If we let him go on thus, every one will believe in him, and the Romans will come and destroy both our holy place and our nation" (John 11:48). By sacrificing a Gali-lean, the Jerusalem authorities might curry favor with their Ro-man overlords.

Caiaphas, like seers of old, spoke more than he knew: "He did not say this of his own accord, but being high priest that year he prophesied that Jesus should die for the nation, and not for the nation only, but to gather into one the children of God who are scattered abroad" (John 11:51f.). Similarly Pilate, Roman co-conspirator with Caiaphas, paid unconscious tribute to the universality of Christ. It was customary for the victim's crime to be placarded on his cross. Pilate "wrote a title and put it on the cross; it read, 'Jesus of Nazareth, the King of the Jews' " (John 19:19). That could serve as warning to any other would-be insur-rectionist who contemplated challenging the authority of Rome. Just to make sure that everybody then in Jerusalem for Passover could read it, the title "was written in Hebrew, in Latin, and in Greek" (John 19:20). Ironically, the three languages sum up the three cultures of which we today are the heirs. Hebrew is the language of religion; Latin the language of law, government, and diplomacy; Greek of literature, drama, and philosophy. Whatever be our concern—personally or professionally—it is lifted high on Christ's cross, at once a monument to our human limitations and shortcomings, and an offering to the Creator God who, for the sake of mutual understanding, made humankind at the beginning to have but one language and one vocabulary (cf. Gen. 11:1).

The Old Testament prophets believed that a Day of the Lord brought in by military might would be a day of gloom and darkness. Now that the kingdoms of the world had given the ultimate demonstration of their power, "there was darkness over the whole land" (Luke 23:44). It proved to be a prelude to the dawning of another era: "And very early on the first day of the week they went to the tomb" and learned that "he is not here; . . . he is going before you" (Mark 16:2, 6f.).

4

Prince of Peace

Pax Romana

Jesus was born into a world at peace. Pax Romana, which everywhere prevailed, was one of the happy circumstances that conspired to aid the spread of the Gospel. In the Forum at Rome, the principal temple of Janus (the god who looked both ways) was one whose gates were always open in time of war, closed in time of peace. They were not closed many times during the life of the empire. Between the legendary Numa, successor to legendary Romulus, and Augustus, they were closed only once. They were closed at the time when Jesus was born: no use then for the power of that deity, the god of beginnings, to go forth against the nation's foes.

Rome was employing those times of repose to consolidate its empire. A spider's web of good roads had been spun across the known world. From Damascus to York, from Constantinople to Cadiz, from the Red Sea to Cologne, the same tough stone surface stretched out before the traveler. And the early Christians did not fail to travel! Irenaeus wrote: "The Romans have given the world peace, and we travel without fear along the roads and across the sea wherever we will." Travel was in some ways easier than today. Paul required no passport, was not subject to electronic baggage inspection, and did not have to get his money changed every time he crossed a national boundary.

If there then prevailed the piping times of peace about which the poets sang, why was Christmas necessary? Why did angels burst in upon the world proclaiming "peace on earth to men of

44

good will"? Note that that is the correct rendering of Luke 2:14. The seventeenth-century translation, "on earth peace, good will toward men," was based upon a text corrupted by copyists. The Greek is correctly translated, "Glory to God in high heaven, and on earth peace among men of God's good pleasure." This reading has been confirmed by the Dead Sea Scrolls. There were, of course, no New Testament documents in the caves, but the phrase "sons of his [i.e., God's] good pleasure" occurs several times in connection with the promised reign of peace. To the ones "chosen of his good pleasure" there is the promise of "eternal peace," "bountiful peace," and the "times of peace." In one of the hymns we read: "How mighty is His power, How plenteous His love to all who do His will."

And there *are* people of good will whose only purpose is God's good pleasure. They are the ones through whom the affairs of persons and nations are fashioned to the end that peace may cover the earth as the waters cover the sea. The angelic hymn is not merely a sentiment to be used on greeting cards; it is enunciation of the principle by which God rules the world. It is not merely a Christmas carol; it is a Christmas revelation. It is not merely a pastoral symphony; it is a governmental policy.

We need not, however, be expert in textual criticism to realize that the first Christian hymn was not a bland assurance of "peace on earth, good will toward men." There were many for whom the first Christmas was not a time of good will. It was hardly a happy time for Herod. Alarmed at this threat to the kind of kingship for which he and his dynasty stood, he did not celebrate Christmas by smiling benignly on all his subjects and wishing them "Happy Holiday!" Instead, he "was in a furious rage, and he sent and killed all the male children in Bethlehem and in all that region who were two years old or under" (Matt. 2:16).

Not exactly a time of "peace on earth, good will toward men" in Bethlehem and environs. Was the first Christmas a time of general rejoicing? Simeon saw that for many of the important people of the world the birth of this child was ominous: ". . . this child is set for the fall and rising of many in Israel, . . . that thoughts out of many hearts may be revealed" (Luke 2:34f.). Not really a merry Christmas for the great ones who lorded it over their fellows, nor for those whose secret thoughts would, under

Christ's discerning, be brought forcibly to attention.

Was it a wholly happy day for the mother of Jesus? "When a woman is in travail she has sorrow, because her hour has come; but when she is delivered of the child, she no longer remembers the anguish, for joy that a child is born into the world" (John 16:21). But was even this latter joy, for her, unclouded? How much did she know of the reception her Boy would meet with in the world? Holman Hunt pictures the cross in the carpenter shop. At close of day, Joseph's youthful apprentice stretches in weariness, and the shadow of a cross falls across the workbench. Did it lie even across the manger? Was this what Simeon meant (Luke 2:34f.) when he said to Mary, ". . . this child is set . . . for a sign that is spoken against (and a sword will pierce through your own soul also)"?

There are those who look back nostalgically to Pax Romana as the golden age of civilization. One has heard people say that what America needs now is something comparable to the Roman army to maintain law and order everywhere. A historian declares that "the Roman world remains our clearest working guide to peace on a large scale." Admittedly, world peace comes only through world organization. This, however, cannot be achieved by conquest but only by consent and cooperation.

Pax Romana—but was it really peace? War was not raging, but is peace simply the absence of war? Pax Romana embraced a great multitude of people, none of whom enjoyed the right of self-determination. Everyone was ultimately subject only to the emperor. To keep a semblance of dominion over his vast domain, the emperor had to have mighty armies. Moreover, this society rested upon slavery, with some to do all the dirty work, while others, wearied with their leisure, turned to gladiatorial combats for amusement. Is this peace? Say, rather, that it was a mere semblance of tranquillity, hiding a reality of injustice, oppression, and misery.

The Biblical Concept of Salvation

Into that grim and volatile situation, One was born whom the church, ever alert to the fulfillment of prophetic dreams, chose to call Prince of Peace (cf. Isa. 9:6). In unexpected ways, that One fulfills and transcends Old Testament expectations about the Messiah. The prospective parents are told, ". . . you shall call his name Jesus, for he will save his people from their sins" (Matt. 1:21). Coming to us through the Latin and Greek, *Jesus* is the equivalent of the Hebrew *Yehoshua*, "God is salvation." Patriotic fervor at the time of the Maccabees had made it a fairly common name. There is more than one Jesus in the New Testament. At Matthew 27:17 some Greek texts contrast Jesus Barabbas with Jesus who is called Christ. Colossians 4:11 mentions Jesus Justus.

In the Old Testament it is principally God who is Savior. Psalm 106:21 recounts how Israel in the wilderness "forgot God, their Savior, who had done great things in Egypt." Found in only thirty-two of the thirty-nine books of the Old Testament, the concept of God as Savior finds its most frequent and distinctive usage in Isaiah of the Exile: "I am the Lord your God, the Holy One of Israel, your Savior" (Isa. 43:3). "I am the Lord, and besides me there is no savior" (43:11; cf. 45:15, 21; 49:26; 60:16; Hos. 13:4). God who is Savior sometimes appointed men to be his agents in salvation, and they are themselves called "savior" or those who "saved" (2 Kings 13:5; Isa. 19:20; Neh. 9:27; Judg. 2:16; Obad. vs. 21).

In the apocryphal literature the term "savior" is applied to two of Israel's military heroes. In Ecclesiasticus 46:1, Joshua is called "a great savior of God's elect" and in 1 Maccabees 9:20f., Judas Maccabaeus, at his death, is mourned as "the savior of Israel." Though human saviors appear at certain crises in Israel's history, "savior" is in the Old Testament nowhere an attribute of Messiah. The scarcity of New Testament references to Jesus as Savior may be due to this, as well as to the fact that references to God as Savior have to do with situations of conflict.

In the Old Testament, salvation, conjoined with peace (cf. Isa. 52:7), is God's glorious deliverance from trouble, bondage, captivity, annihilation. In the New Testament salvation means deliverance from whatever threatens: shipwreck, imprisonment, disease, and sin; rescue of everything that is lost (cf. Luke 19:10): time, energy, character, economic schemes or social systems. It is not until the Prince of Peace has made his impact upon the be-

loved community that 1 John 4:14 can affirm, "And we have seen
and testify that the Father has sent his Son as the Savior of the
world."

In ancient Israel it was believed that truth should be proclaimed
from mountain heights. Setting forth ways in which the gospel
goes beyond the law, the Prince of Peace "went up on the mountain" (Matt. 5:1), promising the happiness of God's children to
those for whom peacemaking is vocation. The ultimate in
Godlike character is set forth in the climactic Beatitude: "Blessed
are the peacemakers, for they shall be called sons of God" (Matt.
5:9).

Christian Peace in a Militaristic World

In the letter to the Romans, Paul strikingly contrasts the Prince
of Peace with Pax Romana. The New Testament word for peace is
eiréne, which has given us such English words as irenic, irenics,
and irenical, as well as the name Irene. *Eiréne* was the Greek
goddess of peace, to whom the Romans gave the name Pax. In art
she was represented as a youthful female, her left hand cradling a
cornucopia, her right hand holding out an olive branch. *Eiréne*
was worshiped in Athens and in Rome. Vespasian built a magnifi-
cent temple dedicated to her. Of all that, Paul makes much in the
letter he writes to people living in Rome. In the New Testament
world Greek was the lingua franca, and Paul uses it in all his
letters.

To citizens dwelling in the capital of an empire that worshiped
Mars (Greek: Ares) as well as *Eiréne,* Paul quotes the prophetic
insight, "the way of peace they do not know" (Rom. 3:17, quoting Isa. 59:8). For a city whose goddess carried an olive branch,
Paul fashions his horticulturally curious analogy of grafting a
wild olive, so that it might "share the richness of the olive tree"
(11:17). "Remember," he emphasizes, "it is not the branches that
support the root, but the root that supports the branches."

To a city that celebrated military triumphs with riotous festivals, Paul points out that "the kingdom of God does not mean
food and drink but righteousness and *eiréne* and joy in the Holy
Spirit" (Rom. 14:17). The Romans sought peace by master-
ing the world, grinding down all "lesser breeds," with legions

tramping the streets where Jesus lived. To Roman Christians, Paul writes, "Let us then pursue what makes for *eiréne* and for mutual upbuilding" (Rom. 14:19).

By the time he concludes the letter, the apostle has captured for the Lord of all countries every good thing for which *eiréne* stood, and given Christendom a glorious new phrase: "The God of *eiréne* be with you all" (Rom. 15:33); ". . . the God of *eiréne* will soon crush Satan under your feet" (16:20). The Prince of Peace revealed the God of Peace who offers us "the peace of God," a peace "surpassing all human ingenuity" (Phil. 4:7; translation suggested by C. E. Raven in *Reconciliation*, March 1936, p. 61).

It is against this background that we must interpret all allegedly militaristic words of Jesus, such as "Do not think that I have come to bring peace on earth; I have not come to bring peace, but a sword" (Matt. 10:34). Jesus is not equipping his followers with a weapon for cutting off the heads of others. Rather, he is announcing that devotion to him sometimes means the severing of earth's dearest relationships. The context makes it clear that this has no reference to external conflict waged with armies and navies and vast weapons of destruction. It is, instead, poignant evidence of the confrontation that the gospel may set up within the family: "I have come," Jesus continues (Matt. 10:35), "to set a man against his father, and a daughter against her mother, and a daughter-in-law against her mother-in-law; and a man's foes shall be they of his own household."

Jesus knew whereof he spoke. Those who think that the Messiah will come and transform the world by a wave of the magic wand are sadly mistaken. On one occasion his own mother and brothers broke up a meeting he was addressing. Because the crowd was so great they could not get to him, they sent a messenger, to whom Jesus replied, "For whoever does the will of my Father in heaven is my brother, and sister, and mother" (Matt. 12:50). Luke 12:51 has it: "Do you think that I have come to give peace on earth? No, I tell you, but rather division." What grief it must have brought Jesus to feel the necessity for making a pronouncement like that!

"He who above all others, wishes to establish friendship and brotherly love among men, must create strife and division."[1] All this reflects, as does so much else in Jesus' ministry, his familiarity with the Old Testament prophets. The burden Jesus felt in having to introduce divisions among people is paralleled in the experience of Jeremiah, who underwent a similar struggle, in the words of John Skinner, "between fidelity to his prophetic commission and the natural feeling and impulses of his heart."[2] Skinner translates Jeremiah 20:9: "If I said, 'I will seek to forget Him, and speak no more in His name,' Twas like glowing fire in my breast, Shut up in my bones. I was weary with keeping it under; I could not hold out."

Also, the mathematics of the divisions within households indicates that Old Testament passages were in Jesus' mind. "In one house," he says (Luke 12:52), ". . . three against two and two against three." That is to say, the two members of the older generation will be against three members of the younger: father and mother on one side; son, daughter, and daughter-in-law on the other. Micah had experienced something similar in his own time: "the son treats the father with contempt, the daughter rises up against her mother, the daughter-in-law against her mother-in-law; a man's enemies are the men of his own house" (Mic. 7:6).

Jesus' conception of the inevitably divisive nature of his work is in contrast to the popular expectation regarding the dawn of the Messianic Age. Elijah would usher it in by turning "the hearts of fathers to their children and the hearts of children to their fathers" (Mal. 4:6). These concluding words of the Old Testament disclose how Jesus reversed current expectations about the coming of the kingdom—not universal acceptance and rejoicing, but division and controversy even within households.

Jesus required people to stand up and be counted. They must be either for him or against him: "He who loves father or mother more than me is not worthy of me; and he who loves son or daughter more than me is not worthy of me" (Matt. 10:37; cf. Luke 9:59–62; 14:26). While the Fourth Gospel has no dominical pronouncement about the divisions Jesus brings, it repeatedly points out that divisions—his word is *schísma*, our English "schism"— did follow his words and deeds (7:43; 9:16; 10:19). Jesus' demands led to differing responses: only so could the faithful and worthy followers be separated from the fickle and fainthearted.

Statements such as "He who is not with me is against me" (Luke 11:23), and the resultant sorting out between friend and foe, produced a schism inside the procurator's palace. While Pilate was trying everything he could think of to dispose of the unhappy situation in which the arrest of Jesus had placed him, his wife sent word to him, "Have nothing to do with that righteous man, for I have suffered much over him today in a dream" (Matt. 27:19).

Disposing of judicial cases before Roman magistrates was not woman's work, and Pilate's wife must have had extraordinary motivation for her intervention. Evidently she had prior knowledge of Jesus. Was she perhaps a secret disciple? In any case, the early church knew her as Procla or Claudia Procula. While her husband, according to tradition, tried ever after on Good Friday to wash his hands of the whole thing, she went on to become a saint.

The sword that Jesus brought was not one the Pentagon would know how to wield, so we must understand other passages sometimes used to enlist Jesus in the service of the military. Did Jesus not use force to cleanse the temple of its defilers? Did he not "drive out those who sold, saying to them, 'It is written, "My house shall be a house of prayer"; but you have made it a den of robbers' " (Luke 19:45f.)? His "weapon," however, was a bundle of rushes used for bedding down the cattle. It is a far cry from that to an atomic blast. In any case, it appears to have been only the cattle upon which he exercised "violence."

A handful of straw certainly could not intimidate the commercial interests bold enough to turn the Father's house into a den of thieves. Why, then, did the merchants scurry away? Jerome says, "A certain fiery and starry light shone from his eyes and the majesty of Godhead gleamed in his face." This is rather like the psalmist's account (44:3) of the entrance into Canaan: "not by their own sword did they win the land, . . . but thy right hand, and thy arm, and the light of thy countenance." Goodness has an ally in every person's breast, and it was conscience that made cowards of the cattlemen. It was this, rather than any show of physical force, which caused their hasty retreat. Since it was the court of the Gentiles that was corrupted, Jesus, in restoring it to its original intention, made a protest on behalf of international goodwill.

In Israel's early history, no distinction can be made between tools and weapons. An ax, used for felling trees and shaping lumber, could be used to ward off wild beasts. The slingshot could be used for bringing down a Philistine giant (cf. 1 Sam. 17:4ff.). Daggers could not be distinguished from hunting knives. When Israel was oppressed by Moab, Ehud, a left-handed Benjaminite, carefully fashioned himself a dirk, some fifteen inches long and easily concealed beneath his clothes. Assigned to carry Israel's tribute to Moab's fat king Eglon, Ehud, having delivered the tribute money, gained access to the king privately and thrust his dirk into the king's stomach; "and the hilt also went in after the blade, and the fat closed over the blade" (Judg. 3:21f.). Thereupon, Ehud summoned the Ephraimites to follow him against the leaderless Moabites, of whom they slew ten thousand (3:29).

A weapon-tool similar to a dirk or dagger is used in many cultures. African schoolboys, for instance, often cut the grass with a panga, a curved blade smaller than a scythe. This throws light on a strange saying attributed to Jesus. On his last night with his friends, he said, " '. . . let him who has no sword sell his mantle and buy one.' . . . And they said, 'Look, Lord, here are two swords!' And he said to them, 'It is enough' " (Luke 22:36, 38). This saying has long troubled the church. Can we really believe that words like these were spoken by the Prince of Peace?

One of the ancient versions of this account contains a different reading. In place of "Let him who has no sword sell his mantle and buy one," it has "Love your enemies"—and that would seem to be more in character for the Savior of the world on the eve of cross-bearing. The men of his time, too, carried a short sharp knife—dirk, dagger, panga—useful in warding off wild animals and for as many domestic purposes as a Boy Scout knife. About to confront the might of the Roman empire, symbolized by Pilate and his minions, Jesus wants to drive home the point his friends seem to have missed, namely, that his sword is truth, his shield is love, he needs no armies. In a moment of melancholy playfulness, he assures them that two small knives—one for Israel, one for Rome—will be all they need to conquer the kingdoms of the world.

So far is war and its violence from the mind and heart of Christ that he can use these military metaphors, confident, that no one can—as has so often happened in the modern world—misunderstand or misinterpret them. Pursuit of peace is continually challenged by those who know neither the Scriptures nor the power of God. "After all," they insist, "Jesus said there would always be wars and rumors of wars." This careless misreading of the Scriptures has done irrevocable harm. What Jesus said was, "And when you hear of wars and rumors of wars, do not be alarmed." This is from the thirteenth chapter of Mark (vs. 7), a passage known to scholars as "the Little Apocalypse." Apocalyptic is a form of literature as characteristic of Hebrew life and thought as drama was of Greek. The word "apocalypse" means uncovering or unveiling. Its purpose is neither to madden nor to mystify but to make clear.

In times of crisis, Hebrew authors invoked powerful, often disturbing imagery to depict changes that they believed to be impending. Such changes, it was hoped, would, after the collapse of the old order, usher in a new and better age. Apocalypse was directed not to the far future, but to some immediate situation (cf. Rev. 1:1, 3; 22:6). Mark's Little Apocalypse weaves some of the sayings of Jesus into a typical tract for the times. The situation to which it addresses itself is one in which the very existence of the beloved community is threatened by the sack of Jerusalem. The passage begins with the disciples marveling at the size of the stones used in constructing the Jerusalem temple: "Look, Teacher, what wonderful stones and what wonderful buildings!"—country boys come to town! Galilean fishermen had nothing like that in the countryside they knew. Jesus responded, "There will not be left here one stone upon another." This happened—quite literally—in A.D. 70, when Roman troops despoiled the city and vandalized the temple, leaving only a few stones intact; these constitute today's wailing wall. When Jesus spoke, the gathering war clouds already cast their shadow.

The Little Apocalypse aims to prepare believers for survival in that impending international crisis. The "desolating sacrilege" (vs. 14) will be set up where it ought not to be. About 168 B.C., the Syrian king Antiochus had desecrated the temple, sacrificing pigs upon its altar to show his utter contempt for Judaism. That was the original "abomination of desolation." Now, in Jesus' time, Pilate had ordered his military banners, replete with Roman eagles, into the temple, in effect setting up idols in the very house of the Lord of heaven and earth. Soon Caligula would be proclaiming himself a god and setting up an image of himself.

The Little Apocalypse circulated among the Christians, as verse 14 reveals: "let the reader understand." When the temple is invaded, and the ultimate blasphemy is achieved, "let those who are in Judea flee to the mountains." This did take place: in order to escape destruction at the hands of the legions of Tiberius, the Christian community did flee to the hills of Gilead, across the Jordan, and establish themselves in Pella, one of the cities of the Decapolis. Against that background Jesus says to his little company: "When you hear of wars and rumors of wars, do not be alarmed—don't panic!" He is not predicting the inevitability of war to the end of time. If he were, he would be denying the kingdom that he had come to establish and in the proclamation of which he gave his life.

At times of crisis people, eager to find some way out, are easily misled, and charlatans quick to take advantage of the anxiety and uncertainty. Jesus warns about that in Mark 13:5: "Many will come in my name, saying, 'I am he!' and they will lead many astray." There were false Christs then, as there are false Christs now. Do not be led astray by any of these, whether they call themselves Jim Jones or Sung Myung Moon. Do not be misled, either, by those who tell you that the Little Apocalypse has to do with "last things." Verse 30 says that "this generation [that is, Jesus' generation] will not pass away before all these things take place." In any case, concern about "last things" can lead us astray from first things, which must always be our concern: doing justice and loving mercy and walking humbly with God.

Although the word was never upon Jesus' lips, talk of Armageddon is another way by which people can be distracted from things that always matter, and so be led astray. It is curious that Armageddon should be so much talked about, because in the whole of the Scripture it occurs only once. In the ancient manuscripts it is spelled in several different ways, so that no one now is quite sure how to spell it. We can, however, try to understand it. The Apocalypse at the end of the Bible depicts in cosmic terms the struggle joined between Christian community and Roman tyranny. The forces of good and evil are to be "mustered at the spot called Harmagedon" (Rev. 16:16, M).

The word not only occurs nowhere else, but no geographer, ancient or modern, has ever located a spot by that name. Some think it a corruption of the Hebrew, meaning either "the desirable city" or "his fruitful mountain"; either of these would refer to Zion. There is in the Old Testament a place called Megiddo. When the Hebrews invaded Canaan, they did not dislodge the inhabitants of Megiddo (cf. Judg. 1:27). At Megiddo, Deborah and Barak battled the forces of Sisera, leader of a Canaanite coalition (cf. Judg. 5:19). In modern times, archeologists have unearthed at Megiddo the stables where Solomon housed his cavalry. A tragic event in Hebrew history occurred when the good king Josiah, ignoring the threat of Pharaoh Neco, went out of his way to join battle with him, and was killed at Megiddo (cf. 2 Kings 23:29).

For these reasons, Megiddo acquired among Hebrews something of the connotation that Waterloo now has for us. Waterloo is a Belgian community where, in 1815, a combined British and German force ended the regime of Napoleon. But Waterloo now has become a symbol, shorthand for any crushing defeat. Megiddo was for Hebrews what Waterloo is for English-speaking people. What has Megiddo to do with Armageddon? The Hebrew "Harmagedon" means "Hill of Megiddo," and many etymologists believe that this is the origin of the term. The difficulty is that Megiddo is on a plain; if there is thought of a hill, it must be of a hill somewhere in the vicinity. Scholarship has no final conclusion.

In any case, the derivation of Armageddon is not of primary importance. It was and is the symbol of cosmic conflict between good and evil, not the name of a land-based battle we are about to witness. It is symbolic of the clash not between armies but between powers and principalities—and the New Testament does not doubt that victory has already been decided! Martin Luther's hymn perfectly catches the mood and the meaning:

> And though this world with devils filled
>   Should threaten to undo us;
> We will not fear, for God hath willed
>   His truth to triumph through us;
> The Prince of Darkness grim,
>   We tremble not for him;

His rage we can endure
For lo! his doom is sure,
One little word shall fell him.

It is interesting to think of the uses to which "Armageddon" has been put. At one time in American history it was a political slogan and battle-cry. When Theodore Roosevelt formed the Progressive party, accepted its nomination for president, and ran for a third term, he damned "special interests" and "moneyed privilege." Roosevelt declared, "We fight in honorable fashion for the good of mankind; fearless of the future, unheeding of our individual fortunes; with unflinching hearts and undimmed eyes; we stand at Armageddon, and we battle for the Lord." In the *New York Times* for February 2, 1980, Billy Graham is quoted: "I think the world stands almost on the edge of Armageddon."

Let these four strange syllables, hurled at us by politicians and cultists, not mislead. Let us, rather, heed the words of the Little Apocalypse: "Watch!" for you do not know at what hour you may have to face some demonic crisis, and there is no longer any time for making ready. ". . . what I say to you, I say to all: Watch" (Mark 13:37). The early church lived in awareness that the present is the only time we really have. Paul writes to the Philippians (4:5), "The Lord is *éggus.*" *Éggus*, which means "near," may be used as the English word is, in both a temporal and a spatial sense.

Jesus reminded his friends that when the fig tree "puts forth its leaves, you know that summer is near" (Matt. 24:32); "near" in this context plainly refers to time. When Paul says, "The Lord is near," successive ages have insisted that he means the Lord is soon to reappear. But "near" has also a spatial sense: Fort Worth is near Dallas; Lake Forest is near Chicago; Tampa is near St. Petersburg. In this sense, "The Lord is near" means that he is close by. Psalm 145:18 assures us that "the Lord is near to all who call upon him, to all who call upon him in truth." In Philippians, Paul no doubt meant what he did in Athens when he said of the Eternal that "he is not far from each one of us" (Acts 17:27).

A prayer of the Anglican Church perfectly captures this sense of "nearness": "Eternal God, who committest to us the swift and solemn trust of life; since we do not know what a day may bring forth, but only that the hour for serving thee is always present, may we wake to the instant claims of thy holy will, not waiting for tomorrow, but yielding today." The first Christians lived in constant awareness of the immediacies and uncertainties of life. "The appointed time," says Paul (1 Cor. 7:29) "has grown very short." The Johannine literature strikes the same note: "And the world passes away, and the lust of it; . . . it is the last hour" (1 John 2:17f.).

It is neither politicians nor cultists but scientists who have now set Armageddon in the forefront of concern. "Atomic fission," says one, "is the diabolical machine at the heart of our civilization, ticking off a few days of grace." Peter Bassell writes: "Atomic plant operation creates small—no one is certain how small—chances of big disasters, accidents in which thousands of lives would be lost. Such pacts with the devil are not unique; the world has been coexisting with Armageddon since 1945."[3] Harrison E. Salisbury says, "Our [that is, American] power can be employed to insure Russia's victory, to insure China's victory, or to prevent Asian armageddon."[4] (For him the word has become so commonplace as not even to require a capital letter.)

The New Testament knows that we always exist in proximity to disaster. In 2 Peter 3:10 we read that "the day of the Lord will come like a thief, and then the heavens will pass away with a loud noise, and the elements will be dissolved with fire, and the earth and the works that are upon it will be burned up." Although that was written in another time, atomic fission has infused it with new and terrifying possibilities. Our continuing preparation for war— not to mention Three Mile Island—may hasten its realization. The symbolic doomsday clock operated by the Bulletin of Atomic Scientists was in January 1980 advanced from nine minutes to seven minutes before midnight!

In the White House basement there is something called the Situation Room, which constantly monitors impending disaster. The room is replete with computer terminals and rotating trays of Top Secrets. On November 9, 1979, doomsday very nearly overtook us—through mechanical error. A "war game" (such fun!) tape was loaded into the NORAD computer in Colorado Springs, Colorado, as part of a computer test. The tape, simulating a missile attack upon North America, was inadvertently transmitted to

America's highly sensitive early warning system. According to the *New York Times* of November 10, 1979, "It took six minutes, during which the nation was in a low-level state of nuclear war alert, to discover the mistake."

All these frightful images make us realize that man-made Armageddon is always just around the corner! God has committed to us the swift and solemn trust of life, and we must not fritter it away in pacts with the devil: "Behold, now is the acceptable time; behold, now is the day of salvation" (2 Cor. 6:2).

He who said that, of all God's children, peacemakers are most akin to the divine nature, had much to say about how peace is to be made.

5

Satan versus Satan

What Is Security?

Two of Jesus' parables have to do with making war and guaranteeing security. One tells of a king whose territory is threatened with invasion by an army said to number 20,000. Since the king has at his disposal only 10,000 troops, he has to weigh carefully whether he would have any chance of success. If not, instead of suicidally joining battle, he will send ambassadors to sue for peace. That the terms may be drastic is suggested by the application Jesus makes to Christian discipleship: "whoever of you does not renounce all that he has cannot be my disciple" (cf. Luke 14:31–33). William Manson thinks the principal lesson of this is that Jesus "needs not camp followers but soldiers."[1]

The other parable has to do with a man who thinks that he can secure his possessions by arming himself to the teeth. "When a strong man, fully armed, guards his own palace, his goods are in peace" (Luke 11:21). The catch is that there really is no security this way, "for when one stronger than he assails him and overcomes him, he takes away his armor in which he trusted, and divides his spoil" (11:22). The punch line here is "He who is not with me is against me" (11:23). In the battle between good and evil, no one can be neutral.

Those who relegate Jesus to the "spiritual" assume that parables like these cannot possibly have any prudential wisdom, any sound advice for a world frantically seeking to increase its security by fabricating fabulous new weapons. So we are told that the strong man is Satan (cf. Isa. 49:24–26), and the stronger man is

Christ (cf. Col. 2:15); and that the king with 20,000 troops is Satan. This is to transform parable into allegory and to create additional problems: Can we really suppose that Jesus is suggesting that our resources are so slender that there are occasions when we should somehow come to terms with Satan?

To avoid this difficulty, others propose that the king with 20,000 troops is God. Are we then to infer that humankind's capacity in confronting Him with whom we have to do is half (10,000) of what God's is? (cf. Matt. 18:24, 28). In the case of the strong man armed, we are told that the "goods" which he intends to safeguard are "souls which Satan has taken captive" and that "Christ makes the powers of hell work together for the good of the faithful."

Certainly we may grant that Jesus' overriding consideration always is that, at whatever cost or hazard to ourselves, we should join the kingdom of light against the kingdom of darkness, the kingdom of love against the kingdom of indifference, the kingdom of God against the kingdom of Satan. At the same time, Jesus took his illustrations from a society in which there were rash national leaders, foolish wars, and a frantic quest for a phantom security. It is basic to the teaching of Jesus that "the sons of this world [or age] are wiser in their own generation than the sons of light" (Luke 16:8). We venture to think, therefore, that, when Jesus discusses the inadequacy of armaments as a means of protection and the folly of going to war with no possible chance of achieving anything good, he has something to say to an age that is spending more than a billion dollars every day trying to ward off the enemy.

The original charter of what is now Columbia University, in New York City, required that the president be an Anglican. When General Dwight D. Eisenhower was chosen for that office, a reporter—hearing that he was not only not an Anglican but not a member of any other religious community—asked whether he was a "religious" man. "I am," he replied, "the most deeply religious man I know; nobody could go through as many battles as I have without faith." When the general was asked what his favorite biblical passage was, he replied: "When a strong man, fully armed, guards his own palace, his goods are in peace" (Luke 11:21).

Concerning that Scripture passage, we need first to understand that it is military property which is under the protection of the heavily armed man. The Greek pictures a warrior in full panoply, armed from head to toe, keeping watch on his headquarters. It would be preposterous to expect all our citizens to deck themselves out in that way—and if they did, theirs would be a community in which no one would want to live. The peace of any decent neighborhood is preserved in quite different ways.

Further, it is not an ordinary human habitation that Jesus pictures as protected thus. The term *aulé,* originally meaning the courtyard around which an extensive residence was built, is vividly translated "palace" or "castle." If that is what is meant, then one man, however heavily armed he might be, could hardly guarantee its security. Actually, Jesus appears to be poking fun at the whole idea of trying to protect oneself by fortification. After picturing the man ridiculously armed to protect his goods, Jesus goes on to add words that General Eisenhower overlooked. (He stopped reading too soon): "but when one stronger than he assails him and overcomes him, he takes away his armor in which he trusted, and divides his spoil" (Luke 11:22). He loses not only his goods but the military equipment he had built up to protect them.

Actually, the strong man armed does not need to wait for a man still more strongly armed to take away his goods. Many a strong man has been defeated by someone who had no money to buy weapons. Guerrilla forces, armed with hand grenades and homemade weapons, have made life miserable for the great empires of earth. British colonial troops in North America were taught to march and stand in rows. They were no match for Indians who hid in forests and ravines. Because of his knowledge of European military tactics and his reputation as a stern disciplinarian, the British made General Braddock, in 1755, commander in chief for North America. Crossing the Monongahela River with 1,400 British regulars and 700 colonial militiamen, he was attacked by a force of fewer than 900 men under Daniel Beaujeu, and had four horses shot out from under him before he was mortally wounded. His army sustained more casualties than there were men in the enemy forces.

In more recent times, Eduardo Mondlane and his patriotic allies made life so miserable for the Portuguese in Mozambique that they had to get out. So also in Kenya and Rhodesia: peoples' armed forces, without benefit of technology and with only the most primitive equipment, "defeated the imperialistic forces armed with modern airplanes, tanks, heavy artillery, and armies. 'Amateurs' who were never trained in any military school have eventually defeated 'professionals' graduated from military academies."[2]

With most of the world's one-time colonies now independent and self-governing, the superpowers do not appear to be in danger from guerrilla forces. Their danger is of quite a different sort. Jesus also has a word for them: "How can Satan cast out Satan?" If peace, as the rabbis said, embraces all the good in the world, then war is the quintessence of all the evil in the world. It literally violates every one of the Ten Commandments: (1) The state replaces God as the one unquestioned object of devotion. (2) The flag becomes an idol, the image before which all other idols must bow down. (3) Each side invokes the name of God:

> God heard the embattled nations sing and shout:
>   Gott strafe England! God save the king!
> God this, God that, God the other thing!
>   Good God! said God, "I've got my work cut out."

(4) Hebrew armies once rested on the Sabbath, but when the Syrians chose that day for a devastating attack, they gave up trying to keep the day holy in wartime. (5) No matter if the soldier pretends to be fighting for the honor of father and mother, it is not a way for him to live long in the land. (6) Not only is the soldier required to kill, but is taught that in warfare it is not murder. (7) The sanctity of the home disappears when chaplains pass out contraceptives to soldiers off duty. (8) To steal the enemy's secrets is considered as honorable as to steal a competitor's markets and to steal goods on the high seas. (9) Truth is the first casualty in any war; persons led to believe they are fighting for freedom and democracy would be reluctant to go if they were told that they were fighting for oil and rubber, manganese and uranium. (10) Wars are not fought to protect the national interest but often for economic reasons: powerful groups covet raw materials and untapped outlets for their products; and power covets power.

The Deadliest Form of Sin

People of the biblical world lived with the idea that there was an organized kingdom of evil, with Beelzebul, "the prince of hell," as ruler of the underground realm, and Satan, "prince and captain of death," constantly going to and fro on earth, breeding enmity, sowing suspicion, spreading lies, encouraging everyone to believe that there is, after all, very little difference between right and wrong.

In the apocryphal Gospel of Nicodemus there is an account of conflict between the two rulers of iniquity. After the crucifixion, Satan returns enthusiastically to Beelzebul to report: "Prepare to receive Jesus of Nazareth, who has done such injury to us and our cause." Beelzebul, however, does not greet this announcement with acclaim. He remembers that Jesus has already snatched Lazarus away from him and is afraid that Satan has overreached himself. "Bring not this person hither," Beelzebul insists, "for he will set at liberty all those whom I hold in prison . . . and will conduct them to everlasting life."

When Jesus does arrive, Beelzebul's direst forebodings come true. As Christ draws near, there is a great shout "as of thunder and the rushing of the winds, saying, Lift up your gates, O ye princes; and be ye lifted up, O everlasting gates, and the King of Glory shall come in." Jesus, "trampling upon death, seized the prince of hell, deprived him of all his power," and led a triumphal procession of the righteous into Paradise. Beelzebul thereupon reproaches Satan: "Our impious dominions are subdued, and no part of mankind is now left in our subjection. . . . O prince Satan, . . . all the advantages which thou didst acquire by the forbidden tree, and the loss of Paradise, thou hast now lost by the wood of the cross."

The church did not include in its canon this Gospel of Nicodemus, although the canonical New Testament affirms: "The reason the Son of God appeared was to destroy the works of the devil" (1 John 3:8). When Jesus not only healed distraught individuals, assumed by their contemporaries to be demon-possessed, but "appointed twelve, to be with him . . . and have authority to cast out demons . . . his friends . . . went out to seize him, for they said, 'He is beside himself' " (Mark 3:14–21). It is not the last time Jesus has been thought crazy.

Investigation of alleged incidents of possession often concluded, not that the person was insane, but that the person might be cooperating with demons: "He is possessed by Beelzebul, and by the prince of demons he casts out the demons" (Mark 3:22). Others in the prophetic tradition had been similarly accused. When John the Baptizer adopted a simple lifestyle to protest the abuses of his time, the people said, "He has a demon" (Matt. 11:18). Jesus' power to restore sanity to the demented was attributed to his being in league with the Archfiend, so that "by the prince of demons he casts out the demons." To that Jesus replied, "How can Satan cast out Satan? If a kingdom is divided against itself, that kingdom cannot stand. And if a house is divided against itself, that house will not be able to stand" (Mark 3:23ff.), to which Matthew appends a third example: "no city. . . divided against itself will stand" (12:25). If Jesus were in league with Satan, he would not be effecting cures that undermined Satan's kingdom. Jesus goes on to say that "whoever blasphemes against the Holy Spirit never has forgiveness, but is guilty of an eternal sin" (Mark 3:29).

In explanation of this saying, Mark adds: "for they had said, 'He has an unclean spirit' " (3:30). Perversion of conscience is, for Jesus, the deadliest form of sin. Their blasphemy lay in attributing the health-giving benefits of his ministry to demonic powers, putting the worst construction on the good deeds of others, willful blindness that will not see. Milton's Satan says, "Evil, be thou my good"; to call good evil and evil good is to demonstrate that one cannot sense the difference between the two. This is the unpardonable sin, unpardonable not because God's forgiveness has been exhausted but because moral turpitude makes it impossible to accept the proffered pardon.

The idea is expressed even more vividly in 1 John 2:11: "But he who hates his brother is in the darkness and walks in the darkness, and does not know where he is going, because the darkness has blinded his eyes." It is possible to remain so long in the gloom and fog of sin as to lose the power of seeing, as mules long detained in mine shafts are deprived of vision. Forgiveness implies a sense of need and an awareness of grace. Those so sunk in moral confusion that they cannot distinguish between light and darkness, good and evil, right and wrong are incapable of opening their hearts to receive God's pardoning love.

Jesus here pronounces a final word about means and ends: we cannot attain a worthy goal by unworthy means or reach a good result by evil methods. Is this not precisely the reason for today's tragic plight of the USSR? When the Bolshevik revolution took place in 1917, the American president welcomed it warmly. Woodrow Wilson, urging Congress on April 2, 1917, to declare war, introduced a cheerful note: "Does not every American feel that assurance has been added to our hope for the future peace of the world by the wonderful and heartening things that have been happening . . . in Russia?

"Russia," Wilson continued, "was known by those who knew it best to have been always in fact democratic at heart. . . . The autocracy that crowned the summit of her political structure . . . was not in fact Russian in origin, character, or purpose, and now it has been shaken off and the great, generous Russian people have been added in all their naive majesty and might to the forces that are fighting for freedom in the world, for justice, and for peace. Here is a fit partner for a League of Honor."[3]

President Jimmy Carter deemed Russia unfit even to host the Olympic Games. What happened? In 1839 the French Marquis de Gustine, traveling in eastern Europe, "denounced the Czar and the Russia which he ruled as a prison house of freedom and oriental despotism and menace to all Europe."[4] Nearly a century and a half later, those who rule Russia are sometimes referred to as "the new Czars." How can this be? What the Bolsheviki aimed at was not an autocratic, dictatorial state: that is what they were rebelling against. What they wanted was democracy. They boasted that they were going to have the most widely based political and industrial democracy on earth. To reach that goal immediately, they decided on a shortcut through undemocratic methods.

Temporarily, they would suppress freedom of speech and press; get rid of dissidents by slaughter or exile; use repression to speed up arrival at a desirable goal. Two generations later, it is clear that violence grows by what it feeds upon. The more you suppress liberty, the more you have to suppress liberty. The more you use tyranny as a method, the more you get tyranny as a result. A Westerner who lived for twelve years in the USSR, persuaded at first that Communism could save civilization, later wrote: "I think the overwhelming weight of historical evidence is to the effect that the means determine the end, and that an idealistic goal, pursued by brutal methods, has a tendency to disappear from view." In other words, we cannot by Satan cast out Satan!

Even churchpeople find this hard to learn. William T. Manning, a Briton who became bishop of the Episcopal Diocese of New York, was an early and ardent advocate of American entrance into World War II; he was one of the few churchpeople who rushed into this position. As early as October 1939 he was calling for "all rightful aid to our allies." In May 1940 he was urging that we "do our utmost" for them; in December of that year he called for "help without stint or limit." In May 1941, when the United States was still more than six months from the firing of a gun, he insisted: "We should now take our full and open part in this conflict."

This stand he based on his belief that freedom and democracy and religion were at stake, and that only by full participation in the war could we hope to preserve them. The bishop evidently did not have a very long memory, because his earlier predictions in this genre were, by events, proved to be ridiculous in the extreme. During World War I, in a speech made in 1918, he proclaimed: "This war is bringing the world into a fellowship and brotherhood that before seemed only a dream. The war begun by military despotism has brought us face to face with the federation of the world. The outcome is to be the sweeping away of autocracy in all its forms and the establishment of democracy and world-wide brotherhood, including to the full those nations at this moment fighting against us.

"Two thousand years ago," he continued, "Jesus Christ gave to the world the message of the brotherhood of man. Today we stand face to face with its realization."[5] Presumably, the burnt child dreads the fire; a bishop who twice thought that by Satan we could cast out Satan should have known better. Some there were, beyond cathderal walls, who learned that Jesus was right.

The Politics of Decency

That human decency is good politics was dramatized for the twentieth century when, following World War I, the victorious allies undertook a repressive treatment of Germany. It was held that Germany's war guilt was so totally reprehensible as to require punishment. But "Germany" is an abstraction. The only way to punish Germany is to make Germans suffer. This the Allies undertook to do, allowing German men, German women, German children to go hungry. This proved self-defeating. In March 1919 Lord Plumer, commander of the British army of occupation, sent a telegram to the War Office, "urging that food should be supplied to the suffering population in order to prevent the spread of disorder as well as on humanitarian grounds."

The telegram emphasized not only what repression was doing to the vanquished, but also what it was doing to the victors. The message described "the bad effect produced upon the British Army by the spectacle of suffering which surrounded them." What had happened was that the British troops insisted on sharing their rations with the women and children among whom they were living, and, as a result, the physical efficiency of the troops had begun to deteriorate.[6] At about the same time the humanitarian leader Herbert Hoover was saying, "You can have vengeance or you can have peace. You cannot have both."

To the end of his life, Woodrow Wilson believed that World War I had achieved the great aims he had in mind in urging the United States to take up arms. On November 11, 1918, announcing to Congress the signing of the Armistice and the cessation of hostilities in Europe, the president said: "We know that the object of the war is attained, the object upon which all free men had set their hearts, and attained with a sweeping completeness which even now we do not realize. Armed imperialism such as the men conceived who were but yesterday the masters of Germany is at an end, its illicit ambitions engulfed in black disaster. Who will now seek to revive it?"[7]

Pleading for the League of Nations in the last speech of his career, at Pueblo, Colorado, on September 25, 1919, Wilson said:

The arrangements of justice do not stand of themselves. . . . they need the support of the combined power of
the great nations of the world. And they will have that support. . . . There is one thing that the American people always rise to and extend their hands to, and that is the truth
of justice and of liberty and of peace. We have accepted that
truth and we are going to be led by it, and it is going to lead
us, and through us the world, out into pastures of quietness
and peace such as the world never dreamed of before.[8]

Writing four decades later, George Kennan took a different
view. Serving diplomatic posts in Europe required him to live for
a quarter of a century with the consequences of the "peace." He
writes: "I hold the first World War to have been *the* great catastrophe of Western civilization in the present century. I think it an
endless pity that it did not cease in 1917, when the Bolsheviki
called for its termination."[9] Again, Kennan writes: "I wonder
whether anyone can read today the literature emanating from the
Western countries in the final year of World War I without feeling
that he is in the presence of a political hysteria so violent that the
real outlines of right and wrong, in so far as they may have existed
at all, are largely lost in the turmoil."[10]

Kennan further notes the long-range effect of all this:

The impression I gain after three or four years of immersion
in these problems is that in attaching such enormous value
to total military victory in 1917 and 1918, the Western people were the victims of a great misunderstanding—a misunderstanding about the uses and effects of the war itself. And
I suspect that this misunderstanding also lies at the heart of
those subsequent developments which have carried the
Western community in the space of forty years from a
seemingly secure place at the center of world happenings to
the precarious and isolated position it occupies today, facing
a world environment so largely beyond its moral and political influence.[11]

Kennan could not understand why, in that situation, the lessons
of World War I were so little remembered by so many, and why the

United States was still supposing that by military might it could overcome Communist ideology. At a time when the Politburo had, in the Western mind, replaced Hitler as the center and source of all evil, the West was still toying with the idea that by Satan it could cast out Satan. Writing with a knowledge of the Soviet people possessed by few this side of Moscow, Kennan is sure that the United States should continue to make a distinction between the Russian people and the Russian rulers. If we sought by military might to destroy the latter, the blow would fall upon the former. He is convinced

> that throughout all these years of anti-capitalist and anti-American propaganda in the Soviet Union, the Soviet people have remained touchingly well-inclined towards the United States, touchingly unwilling to accept the endless efforts of their government to persuade them that Americans meant them harm. You come here to the profound ambivalence in the relation between people and regime in such a country as Soviet Russia: to the fact that the interests and aspirations of these two entities in some ways differ but are in other ways identical, and that it is impossible to distinguish between the two when it comes to the hardships and injuries of war. Outright war is itself too unambivalent, too undiscriminating a device to be an appropriate means for effecting a mere change of regime in another country. You cannot logically inflict on another people the horrors of nuclear destruction in the name of what you believe to be its salvation, and expect it to share your enthusiasm for the exercise.
>
> Such warfare (and this was true even in 1917) involves evils which far outweigh any forward political purpose it might serve—any purpose at all, in fact, short of sheer self-preservation, and perhaps not even short of that. Even if warfare had been the answer to Communism in a different stage of weaponry (and, mind you, I do not think it would), it would certainly not be the answer in the day of the atom.[12]

Kennan was a career diplomat who spoke the language of the country to which he was assigned, and was able to advise the State

Department wisely. More recently, career diplomats have been
passed over in favor of businessmen ambassadors who can
neither speak the language nor see beneath the surface.

Americans now tend to link together Russians and Chinese as
potential enemies. Servants of the church, speaking the language
of the Chinese, report significant encounter with them. From the
life of the missionary family into which she was born, Pearl Buck
recounts an incident revealing the seldom-tried power of nonviolence. Often her parents and their children were the only white
people in the entire area. Once when drought came, the Chinese
blamed the Americans: "the gods are angry because foreigners
have come into the city."[13] Word came that the mob was assem-
bling to slaughter the entire Sydenstricker family. Andrew, husband and father, was away on his itineration. How should the
mother protect and defend herself and the children?

Being a practical woman, she quickly prepared tea and cakes.
"Then when all was ready as though for a feast she swept and
made the room spotlessly neat and set the chairs as for guests.
Then she went to the court and to the front gate and threw it wide
open."[14] She dressed the children and then called to the mob:
"Come in, friends, neighbors, I have tea prepared." She sang to
them a hymn—the mob could not understand how she could be so
calm and unafraid in face of such danger. Presently the leader rose
and said loudly: "There is nothing more to do here. I go home."
That was the signal for all, and soon everything was quiet and
peaceful again. A woman's kindliness had outwitted a mob—and
that night the drought was broken by rain.

Tragically, nations have not much experimented with that on
the grand scale, and in her autobiography Pearl Buck described
what war was doing to her children:

> I who have been reared in one world, a Christian one, and
> taught that love and brotherhood must be the law of life,
> and reared, too, in another world yet kindlier, with the
> Chinese belief that life is sacred and that it is evil to kill even
> a beast, and how much more a human being, I now face the
> tragic possibility that my sons must deny both Christian and
> Asian teaching. They must join our armed forces and fight

perhaps an Asian people, a people whom I love and admire
and to whom I am deeply indebted.[15]

She lived to see that dire prophecy come true in Vietnam, where
American fighting men joined with one group of Vietnamese in
killing Asians.

We Americans seem to think that temperance can be promoted
by increasing the availability of liquor; discipline cultivated by
casting off all restraint; murder ended by murdering the mur-
derer. Visiting an army base on a July afternoon in a command
car driven by a corporal, the writer was invited by his host, a
major, to have a cold drink. Since it is against regulations for a
corporal to fraternize with a major, the driver could not join in the
refreshment. Is it conceivable that so undemocratic an organization could bring in the day of brotherhood?

There is a tense moment in Revelation when, in the right hand
of One seated upon a throne, there is seen a scroll, sealed with
seven seals. The question arises, "Who is worthy to open the
scroll . . . ?" (Rev. 5:2). The seer, deeply troubled because no one
seemed worthy, hears an elder say: "Weep not; lo, the Lion of the
tribe of Judah . . . has conquered, so that he can open the scroll
. . ." (vs. 5). Who better qualified than the conquering lion of the
lionlike tribe? But when one does come who is worthy, it is not a
lion at all, but "a Lamb standing, as though it had been slain"
(5:6).

The Lamb's powerful gentleness has not often been tried by
state or national governments. American history does have a notable but little-known example in the Commonwealth of Pennsylvania. In 1682 William Penn received this land as payment for
an old debt the British Crown owed him. From the white people
the American Indians had already received such ill-treatment that
the atmosphere was charged with hatred and suspicion when
Penn arrived. He was, nevertheless, determined to carry out his
"Holy Experiment." He began by doing an extraordinarily honest
and sensitive thing.

The British king had given Penn title to the land, and with it he
could legally do whatever he wanted. Since the Indians had lived
there from time immemorial, it occurred to him that they had

some rights and claims, too. He paid them for these, making it clear that he would take only what they would knowingly and willingly permit. Another unusual thing he did was not to take advantage, as frontier tradesmen were wont to do, of the Indians' fondness for strong drink. One whose offer of an unworthy deal Penn rejected said, "I believe truly he does aim more at justice and righteousness and spreading of truth than at his own particular gain."

Penn and his Friends made no effort to fortify themselves against the Indians. They built no forts, had no soldiers, no militia, no weapons. It was at a time of wars and rumors of wars. Pennsylvania was still under British rule. There were not only wars between neighboring states and Indians but also between England and France, England and Spain. French and Spanish settlers in the New World were involved, and England needed soldiers for its conflicts. The colonies around Pennsylvania "began to urge that this was the one point that was not armed and that it was a kind of treachery to all the rest" that Pennsylvania would not raise any military force or construct forts or do anything to sustain "the common burden of armaments on which they depended" against those whom they called "the savage and murderous Indians."

Neighbors complained that the colony was "entirely bare to the attacks of the enemies, not a single armed man, nor, at the public expense, a single fortification to shelter the unhappy inhabitants." The Friendly Quakers continued to refuse to prepare for war, praying that they "might continue humbly to confide in the protection of that Almighty power whose providence has hitherto been as walls and bulwarks round about us." The record has it that "for thirty years the Quakers lived in absolute peace. Others were slain, others were massacred, others were murdered, but they were safe. Not a Quaker woman suffered assault, not a Quaker child was slain, not a Quaker man was tortured."

So idyllic was this province that colonists settled there who were not Quakers. Gradually there came to be a majority of those who disapproved of the Quaker principle of nonviolence, and so failed to sense what it was that made the Commonwealth so attractive. When at last, under pressure, the Quakers gave up the government of the state and war broke out, and some Pennsylvanians lost their lives, only three Quakers were killed, and they had all so far forgotten their faith as to have armed themselves with "weapons of defence." The Indians did not recognize as Quakers those who carried guns and had forgotten Jesus' word, "how can Satan cast out Satan?" Sword-carrying Quakers perished by the sword.[16]

Jesus has a great deal more to say along this line.

6

Perish by the Sword

Wielding the Sword

Of all those before him in the prophetic tradition, none influenced Jesus more than Jeremiah. In an oracle on Philistia, picturing the doom in store for it and its neighbors, Jeremiah exclaimed, "Ah, sword of the Lord! How long till you are quiet? Put yourself into your scabbard, rest and be still!" (47:6). Humankind had too long presumed to be wielding the sword of the Lord, and bloodshed was rife. When impulsive Peter cut off the ear of the high priest's servant at Jesus' arraignment before the authorities, Jesus said, "Put your sword back into its place; for all who take the sword will perish by the sword" (Matt. 26:52).

It has too often happened in the case of individuals. Hodding Carter (1907–72) was a distinguished journalist and newspaper publisher whose stand against old southern customs often brought him into conflict with peers and contemporaries. A series of articles on racial, religious, and economic intolerance won him the 1945 Pulitzer Prize for distinguished reporting. Because of the threats leveled at him and his family, he believed that he needed weapons to protect his home.

In a biographical sketch of Carter, Gene Lyons[1] reported that "Guns never brought anything but misery" into the life of Hodding, Sr., "although he never did learn to live without them." His son Philip, while on a hunting trip, accidentally fired a .30-.30 rifle slug through his foot, and was fortunate in getting help at once. "But it was the death of his youngest son, Tommy, at age 19 . . . of a self-inflicted pistol wound while drinking with a girl friend and playing Russian roulette in New Orleans that came as close to crushing his spirit and will as anything ever did."

A great and enduring sorrow of Adlai Stevenson's life was the tragedy of his accidentally killing, at age twelve, his fifteen-year-old cousin. There was a teenagers' party, at which a military academy student was asked to go through the manual of arms. Adlai turned up a .22 rifle. The student thought it empty, and executed his routine to the delight of all. Adlai then took the gun, copied the motions of his sister's friend, the gun went off, and a bullet entered the forehead of Ruth Merwin. The boy was exonerated at the inquest; for forty years he spoke of it to no one, and no one spoke of it to him. Says a biographer: "What effect the accident had . . . upon Adlai Stevenson's character is a matter of surmise."[2]

On a springtime evening, the writer had dinner with a men's Bible class; the president disclosed that he always slept with a loaded revolver under the pillow. The pastor expressed dismay: "Are you not afraid that the gun might go off accidentally, and that the mere possession of it might provoke violence on the part of an intruder?"

"I feel that I must do it," he said. "I owe it to my family to protect them in that way."

That was in May. At 4 A.M. on a September morning, the pastor's telephone rang. It was this man's wife, now suddenly widowed. "Could you please come right over?" she asked. "Someone broke into our house. My husband took his revolver and started down the stairs to protect us—and they killed him."

Since World War II, no one has been killed by nuclear weapons, but since 1945 "conventional weapons" have taken more than ten million lives in wars, revolutions, guerrilla combats, and personal tragedies. It was the United States Army that taught New York's "Son of Sam" to kill, and an army "buddy" who provided his lethal weapon. "It is of little use trying to suppress terrorism," wrote E. F. Schumacher, "if the production of deadly devices continues to be deemed a legitimate employment of man's creative powers."[3] Americans now possess more than 50 million handguns, with the number increasing at the rate of 2.5 million per year. In some sections of our society, handguns are now the leading cause of death, the result being that our murder rate makes the United States "number one." Our "10.2 homicides per 100,000 people compares with 1.3 for Japan; 1.1 for Sweden; 1.0 for Great Britain; 0.9 for France."[4] We seem to be living in the kind of primitive society described by Thucydides: "they passed their ordinary life with weapons like the barbarians."

Even within the military, guns often result in unintended slaughter. "Doughboys" of World War I frankly related that many an officer listed as "Killed in Action" was shot in the back by his own men who resented him. Samuel Eliot Morison's history of the United States Navy in World War II reports that "in many battles the worst damage to the Allied troops was done by their own forces." He cites examples:

> A landing force hitting the beach is bombed and strafed by its own planes, who thought they were making a great score on the enemy. The front-line offensive is shelled by long-range artillery of its own allies who were under the impression that their range was carrying the bombardment just ahead of the army. Men in a submarine are being thrown from side to side to avoid the depth-charges that their own destroyers are dropping. After a while, the men under the worst kind of tension begin to curse and wave their fists at their allies and shout, "Whose side are you on anyway?"[5]

Of World War I it has been said that the only individual who emerged from that era with an enhanced reputation was Jesus of Nazareth. He perfectly analyzed the situation: "all who take the sword will perish by the sword."

If Jeremiah wished the sword put back into its scabbard, he himself set an example of nonresistance. With the Babylonians knocking at the gates of Jerusalem, the prophet said to the king, "Behold I set before you the way of life and the way of death. He who stays in this city shall die by the sword, by famine, and by pestilence; but he who goes out and surrenders to the Chaldeans . . . shall live and shall have his life as a prize of war" (21:8f.).

Imprisoned then for un-Jewish activities, Jeremiah emerged from the dungeon still proclaiming, "If you will surrender . . . , then your life shall be spared, and this city shall not be burned with fire, and you and your house shall live. But if you do not surrender . . . , then this city shall be given into the hand of the

Chaldeans, and they shall burn it with fire, and you shall not escape from their hand" (38:17f.). The prophet had calculated the risk, but the foolish king, Zedekiah, did not sue for peace. Then it happened as the prophet had said. The invaders "broke down the walls of Jerusalem, . . . carried into exile the rest of the people"— except that "they left in the land of Judah some of the poor people who owned nothing" (39:8-10). Jeremiah, too, remained behind (cf. 40:6). Over the community that had scorned Jeremiah's doctrine of nonresistance, a poet sang this dirge:

> How lonely sits the city
>   that was full of people!
> How like a widow has she become,
>   she that was great among the nations!
>   [Lamentations 1:1]

Six centuries later, Jesus wept over the same city. For others, that Palm Sunday was a festive occasion, but when Jesus "drew near and saw the city he wept over it, saying, 'Would that even today you knew the things that make for peace! But now they are hid from your eyes' " (Luke 19:41f.). In predicting that "your enemies will . . . dash you to the ground, you and your children within you, and they will not leave one stone upon another" (Luke 19:43f.), Jesus foresees that the Roman armies will do to Jerusalem what the Babylonian armies did in the time of Jeremiah. Jesus' prediction was fulfilled almost literally in A.D. 70.

The Practicality of Nonviolence

Like Jeremiah, Jesus followed the tactic of nonviolence. It is sometimes urged upon us that the teaching of Jesus is too idealistic and impractical. In his own encounters with hostility, he proved it practical—by practicing it. Following his first sermon in his hometown, those who "had known him" did not congratulate him, or call his words "beautiful," or say they "enjoyed" it. Instead, "they rose up and put him out of the city, and led him to the brow of the hill on which their city was built, that they might throw him down headlong" (Luke 4:29). Was his ministry to end before it had really begun?

Perhaps it would have if he had fought to free himself. Instead, "passing through the midst of them he went away" (Luke 4:30). East African theological students had an existential way of understanding this. It was just after the Mau Mau "emergency," during which Kikuyu tribesmen, determined to oust the British, killed some of their own people who refused to join the movement. Asked how it was that Jesus could have walked away from a mob, some of the students said, "It was a miracle!" Others shouted, "No! No! During the 'emergency' people threatened with death faced their would-be killers so calmly, so courageously, that they put down their weapons and let them walk away!"

Toward the end of his life, Jesus faced another tense situation. Roman soldiers and temple police joined forces to take into custody One who was not trying to escape: Judas took "a band of soldiers and some officers from the chief priests and the Pharisees" (John 18:3). It was a classic example of military overkill. The detachment of soldiers was a cohort, 600 troops of the Roman army of occupation by which the empire sought to preserve law and order in an out-of-the-way province.

The GI gear they had was strangely irrelevant: they came out against Jesus equipped with "lanterns and torches and weapons." This was no doubt standard issue for night-time operations. But it was Passover time. Anyone who has seen the Paschal full moon in Jerusalem knows how torches would fade before its brilliance, lanterns pale into insignificance. Consider whom they were seeking in this fashion. How do you locate the Light of the World with a flashlight? Also, they had weapons—weapons to subdue the Lord of glory! Matthew 26:55 reports that Jesus said: "Have you come out as against a robber, with swords and clubs to capture me?"

He had sat daily in the temple and they did not lay a hand upon him. He was not now hiding from the authorities or trying to run away. He could have had if he wished "more than twelve legions of angels," matching their 600 troops with 50,000 to 70,000 members of the heavenly host! But Jesus does not fight in this way. Instead, he stepped forward and said: " 'Whom do you seek?' They answered him, 'Jesus of Nazareth.' Jesus said to them, 'I am he,' " whereupon "they drew back and fell to the ground" (John 18:4f.).

The police should earlier have learned how poorly equipped

they were to deal with Jesus. There had been a previous attempt to arrest him. When those sent to bring him into custody returned empty-handed, their superiors demanded, " 'Why did you not bring him?' The officers answered, 'No man ever spoke like this man!' " (John 7:45f.). No doubt the strangest excuse a police squadron ever offered for nonperformance of duty! So now, filled with a courage they know not of, Jesus stepped forward, and "they drew back and fell to the ground." Was this but the natural effect of a troubled conscience? Is it not God's will that guilt should ever quail before innocence?

Taken into custody and asked about his allegedly subversive teaching, Jesus replied: "I have spoken openly to the world; . . . I have said nothing secretly. . . . Ask those who have heard me, . . . they know what I said" (John 18:20f.). It was the religious authorities who were questioning him, and by their own law one person's testimony was worthless; it had to be supported by at least one other witness. Not really interested in Jesus' teaching, the inquisitors were trying to provide an occasion for him to incriminate himself. He refused to fall into the trap; whereupon "one of the officers standing by" (John 18:22) gave Jesus a slap in the face, a sharp blow with the open hand.

The startled discomfiture caused by Jesus' reply manifests itself in this burst of self-deceptive fury. After Jesus had been turned over to the execution squad, the soldiers with their barracksroom humor repeatedly came up to him, saying, " 'Hail, King of the Jews!' and struck him with their hands" (John 19:3). But this initial slap in the face was delivered by an officer and a gentleman: "Is that how you answer the high priest?"—and is evidence of how weak the case was against Jesus. When the police have no evidence, they sometimes think they can produce it by brutality.

Jesus' answer was, "If I have spoken wrongly, bear witness to the wrong; but if I have spoken rightly, why do you strike me?" Truth has its own steadfast answer to falsehood, and Jesus makes it without anger or insinuation. Here his example precisely accords with his teaching. To crowds on the mountain he had said, "Do not resist one who is evil. But if any one strikes you on the right cheek, turn to him the other also" (Matt. 5:39). It is no doubt this incident that lies behind "when he was reviled, he did not revile in return; when he suffered, he did not threaten; but he trusted to him who judges justly" (1 Pet. 2:23). A variant reading there has it: "he trusted to him who judges unjustly"—that is, not to the Supreme Magistrate of the universe but to the petty local official who presumed to sit in judgment upon him. In so doing "he committed no sin; no guile was found on his lips. . . . By his wounds you have been healed" (1 Pet. 2:22–24).

The Sword of Corruption

The treatment Jesus suffered at the hands of cruel men is always cause for sober reflection. Deploring what "they" did to him, we recognize, on second thought, that in a sense "they" are "we." How do those who now represent us in the international scene respond to a slap in the face?

The answer to that is, too often, with a show of force, which turns out disastrously. Even "humanitarian" efforts undertaken by the military have sometimes turned out tragically. At his news conference on June 25, 1975, President Gerald Ford was asked how he explained the dramatic rise in his popularity as measured by public opinion polls. He replied: "Obviously the *Mayagüez* incident and the way it was handled has had a good reaction." Surely this was another classical illustration of military overkill. When Russian, Polish, or Japanese fishing vessels get too near our shores, we release them after payment of a fine. The *Mayagüez*, a small ship of the United States merchant marine headed for Thailand, was seized by a Cambodian gunboat.

Cambodia (now known as Kampuchea), a tiny nation of seven million people, with an annual per-capital income of $130, was then ruled by a government that had been in power less than a month. It had already announced its intention to release the *Mayagüez*, but had had so little experience in foreign affairs that it used only the Cambodian language to broadcast notice of the pending release of the vessel. President Ford, ignoring the act of Congress forbidding further use of military power in southeast Asia, sent 1,100 Marines to liberate the vessel and its crew of thirty-nine. The Marines dropped bombs on the wrong island, lost forty-one of their own men killed, with fifty others wounded.

So with President Carter's effort to free the United States diplomatic personnel held hostage in Iran. The European community had reluctantly announced its support of economic sanctions against Iran, with the understanding that there would be no United States military intervention. The president had also announced that no military action would even be considered until after May 11 (Mother's Day!). Further, Congress, uneasy lest some military adventure be afoot, had reminded him of the War Powers Act of 1973, requiring the president to consult with Congress before committing troops anywhere.

Under those circumstances, the president sent some ninety troops, six C-130 transport planes, eight helicopters, and ninety crewmen for rendezvous in the Iranian desert, preparatory to storming the Teheran embassy. Three of the helicopters failed; a fourth crashed into a C-130 (on the ground!). In the ensuing conflagration, eight Americans were burned alive and five more were wounded. The mission was thereupon aborted, and the survivors departed as hastily as they could, leaving behind a burned out C-130, four good helicopters, and the charred remains of eight human beings. The president had up to that time boasted that, during the three years of his presidency, no American had lost his life in military action. The score at Dasht-e-Kavir (Great Salt Desert) was eight dead, five wounded, no hostages rescued.

The brandishing of swords produces corrupt business practices. Following World War I, it was disclosed that arms manufacturers had made a career of selling weapons to both sides in any potential conflict. A sale made in one country would be reported to the other as reason why the latter should purchase still larger quantities. In those days, such vendors were called "Merchants of Death," but the profession has now become quite respectable, with big-power governments themselves as partners. This deadly business, contagious as smallpox, has enormously multiplied since World War II, when big business and big government learned how to enrich each other's coffers.

Following World War II, the United States imposed upon Japan a "Peace Constitution" forever renouncing "war as the sovereign right of the nation," abolishing all land, sea, and air forces. General MacArthur himself sidestepped this with the creation of a 75,000-man National Police Reserve. Between 1970 and 1979 Japanese military expenditures rose from $1.58 billion annually to $10 billion. Except for China, this was larger than the entire national budget of any other country in that part of the world. During the 1980s Japan will acquire from the United States military aircraft—700 F-15 fighters and 45 P-30 antisubmarine planes—at a cost of $4.6 billion.

Irish patriots are sure that weapons dealers could, by ceasing to ply their nefarious trade, reduce hostilities in that country. Betty Williams, one of the two Irish women awarded the Nobel Peace Prize, reports that international gun-runners sell to all para-militaries in her tortured land. Between 1960 and 1975, arms sales to "developing" countries more than doubled. In some Latin lands it was tripled; in some Middle Eastern countries it increased eightfold.

Military spending has everywhere increased faster than the economic base to support it; it has taken ever larger portions of the Gross National Product (GNP); it has resulted in corresponding decline in funds for health, education, and welfare. With the lure of lucrative export opportunities, the United States government has provided generous credit terms for arms transactions, with Military Assistance Advisory Groups in some forty countries doing "their best to sell foreign governments on the merits of American-made weaponry."[6] This entails altering the scale of values and the way of life in lands unaccustomed to "democratic" procedures.

United States foreign policy has too much depended upon our being sword-salesperson to the world! Apart from a larger vision of how true security is to be obtained, international "aid" can be administered in ways that intensify the problem it was intended to solve. In the 1950s and 1960s United States aid to Iran totaled some $2 billion. Iran regards as its primary security interest the safety of the sea lanes through which flows the oil it must export to finance the nation's "development." The United States has carried out an "unprecedented volume of military technological transfers to Iran."[7]

This made a tremendous impact upon a whole society. From five to ten years may elapse between approval of a request for military equipment and its delivery. The interval is used to train and indoctrinate thousands of young men in the care and feeding of weapons. All that accompanied this—American films, music, television, liquor, pornography, sexual casualness—was precisely what enraged Muslim fundamentalists, made American culture unwelcome, and led to the debacle at the United States embassy in Teheran. We taught young Islam to take the sword—but not what Jesus said would be the consequences of so doing.

Quite early in the "game," among editors and cartoonists of Iran, a floppy-eared, bug-eyed jackass replaced the figure of Uncle Sam as symbolizing the United States. The idea seemed to be that we had made ourselves ridiculous in the aid we presumed to render through the Point Four program. We were trying to sell America as a commodity rather than as an ideal. We informed the peoples of Asia and Africa how short a time an American laborer had to work to acquire a pair of shoes, and how many pairs of shoes an American family accumulated in a year. Many Asians and Africans did not wear shoes!

We boasted of our dish washing machines; they had hardly enough dishes to be worth bothering about. We reported the number of American families with two cars in the garage; they walked, rode bicycles, or rode on donkey-back. In lands where the telephone was still a rarity we boasted of the number of radio and television sets. After a 41,000-mile-trip around the world in 1951, Governor Thomas E. Dewey pointed out that all this had played into the hands of the Marxists. Communists would indeed have been glad to subsidize that kind of propaganda.

Continuing United States "aid" to Iran strengthened the position of the Shah, who, in turn, sought to strengthen himself by the suppression of all opposition. Both Ayatollah Khomeini and Abolhassan Bani-Sadr were among the tens of thousands driven into exile. Amnesty International reported in 1977 that Iran had the "highest rate of death penalties in the world, no valid system of civilian courts, and a history of torture which is beyond belief." Estimates of political prisoners ranged from 25,000 to 100,000. The Central Intelligence Agency (CIA) and a U.S. AID program trained SAVAK, the Shah's 40,000-man secret police, in methods for ruthless suppression of dissent. Identification of the United States with the Shah's repressive regime was dramatized in 1973 when Richard Helms, former CIA director, was appointed United States ambassador to Iran.

The Nixon era proclaimed the Shah our best friend and most

dependable ally in the Persian Gulf region, whence comes much of the oil for the motorists of America. The United States not only equipped SAVAK with cattle prods and other equipment used in the "dirty tricks" department, but also provided sophisticated fighter planes and other equipment. By 1976 one-third of Iran's GNP was being spent on weapons; in the years 1974–78 Iran bought $16.3 billion worth of arms from the United States. Iran's normal economy could not afford such extravagance. In order to buy United States arms, therefore, Iran quadrupled the price of oil. Thus the American motorist and the American homeowner paid for the weapons that United States manufacturers sold to the Shah.

As a presidential candidate, Jimmy Carter decried as "cynical" and "dangerous" the United States policy of massive arms sales abroad, and Walter Mondale promised that "a Carter administration will make food, not guns, the major focus of American foreign policy." President Carter, however, continued the sorry business, and what had once been the "arsenal of democracy" became just an arsenal. Although Carter proposed a ceiling on arms sales abroad, the ceiling did not cover arms sales to allies, or the provision of related services, or sales through private firms.

Meanwhile, Iranian anger against the Shah's oppression had mounted to the point where the Peacock Throne was tottering. Until the Shah's actual abdication, however, the CIA was assuring President Carter that the Shah was a stabilizing force in the troubled Middle East and should continue to receive our support. When the exiled Shah required medical treatment, the United States ambassador to Iran warned that to admit him to the United States would have disastrous repercussions in Iran. Under pressure from Henry Kissinger and international bankers, Carter ignored the ambassador's warning and made a great public show of humanitarian concern for a sick man who needed treatment at a New York hospital. A Canadian doctor was imported to perform the operation. The sequel was occupation of the embassy in Teheran, prolonged detention of United States hostages, the aborted rescue attempt, and a future that appeared ominous.

Sword-wielders have not much sense of balanced budgets, and Pentagon expenditures seem to be supervised by drunken sailors. A Defense Department analyst reported that cost overruns in manufacturing the C-5A cargo plane approached $2 billion. The man who blew the whistle was promptly fired (later reinstated at a lower level, he sued Richard Nixon and two aides for ruining his career). Asked about the situation, former President Nixon said that he "paid little attention" to the matter because he was "preoccupied with the Vietnam War and other issues."[8]

In December 1979 President Carter instructed his advisers to seek military bases in the Middle East, with Saudi Arabia, Oman, and Somalia considered possibilities. By April 1980 the United States had concluded military and economic accords with Oman and Kenya, giving American forces access to air and naval bases, with technical arrangements to be worked out. Oman would receive $100 million and Kenya about $50 million. The United States would spend an additional $100 million improving port facilities at Mombasa and Muscat and the airstrip on Masira Island. Negotiations with Somalia, which had been dropped when that nation set the price at $2 billion, were renewed when it was learned that, in return for $77 million in economic aid, $20 million in military credits, $5 million in support money, Somalia would grant the United States access to the port and airstrip at Berbera, strategically located near oil shipping lanes in the Gulf of Aden.

It was also announced that $1 billion would be spent in enlarging and improving the previously acquired United States naval and air bases on British-ruled Diego García in the Indian Ocean. The runway would be widened so as to accommodate B-52 bombers; hangar ramps would also have to be widened. Temporary quarters had already been installed for the 1,750 Americans in support crews previously stationed on the U-shaped island. Although it is 2,300 miles from the Persian Gulf, it is much nearer than the island of Guam, from which long-range sorties had been flying; nearer, too, than Subic Bay in the Philippines, whence food, spare parts, and mail had been dispatched—consuming nobody knows how much gasoline.

By that time, the United States Indian Ocean fleet—two aircraft carriers, sixteen warships, eight supply vessels, and an 1,800-man amphibious force of marines—was causing other problems. The cost of fuel and supplies for a few months had exceeded $1 billion. Human problems were of greater concern.

The aircraft carrier *Nimitz*, for example, had been at sea for more than a hundred days; for the first time since World War I, crewmen were allowed to drink beer on board. Morale for the entire personnel had deteriorated to the point where it placed strains upon the Navy's "capacity to perform missions elsewhere."[9]

The military, too, show small respect for the decencies of society. On February 28, 1980, the army introduced its first new battle tank in twenty years: the XM-1 was described by the chief of staff as "better than anything the Russians have or anything we know they have on the drawing board." The General Accounting Office, after tests, pronounced the new combat vehicle unsatisfactory. This made no difference to the army chief of staff: "I completely disagree with the GAO," he said. The army therefore went on with its plans to "christen" the first tank off the assembly line. Julia Harvey Abrams, widow of General Creighton W. Abrams, "smashed a red, white and blue bottle of champagne over the gun barrel of the Army's new main battle tank, naming it for the late Army Chief of Staff."[10] Since "christen" means "receive into the Christian church by baptism," one wonders what the headline can mean: "Army's New Main Battle Tank Christened." In any case, a few minutes after the "christening," the new tank, showing off for the crowd, got stuck in reverse.

The army made a big thing of expelling from West Point some cadets caught cheating. Yet new recruits report that recruiting agents had given them advance information that would ensure their passing the entrance examination. According to the *New York Times*, in order to meet quotas "recruiters frequently give enlistees test answers, issue forged Social Security cards and tax forms and fabricate recruits' educational qualifications."[11]

Americans do not like to hear about the arms business. It is said that in ancient societies people expressed their resentment at hearing bad news by killing the messenger who brought it. We Americans have the best news-gathering organizations in the history of the world. Yet their policymakers tailor the news to what they think we want to hear. So we remain blind and deaf to those who remind us that Jesus was right when he said that "all who take the sword will perish by the sword."

Ruth Leger Suvard, chief economist for the United States Arms Control and Disarmament Agency, annually produced for the government an account of how national expenditures were being allotted. This was ended in 1972 by Presbyterian elder Melvin Laird, then secretary of defense, who said: "The comparisons between military and social spending were complicating the Pentagon's task of presenting the defense budget to Congress."[12]

The United Nations, founded "to save succeeding generations from the scourge of war," committed to its General Assembly the responsibility for considering "the principles governing disarmament and the regulation of armaments."[13] When Secretary-General Kurt Waldheim in 1977 spoke of the difficulty he experienced in "attempting to reverse the perilous world arms spiral" and called attention to the dangers of military competition and the billions of dollars it was annually taking out of the world economy, his message was neither broadcast nor reported in newspapers.

The New York press that day "gave more attention to the attempt of the City Council to control pornography than to the attempt of the Secretary-General to control a problem which, if left unattended, could make the earth as barren as the moon. "Are we to believe," asks Norman Cousins, "that the issue of human survival is less important than whether a massage parlor should be located 300 or 500 feet from a residential neighborhood?"[14]

American economy is so completely geared to military production that we assume that there is no other way. If we take Jesus seriously, we have to change our minds about how to obtain the kind of society we profess to want, and the kind of jobs we ought to provide. There are better things we can do with swords than wave them menacingly in the sunlight.

7

Swords into Plowshares

We are accustomed to divide Old Testament prophets into two groups: major prophets and minor prophets. When these terms were first bestowed, they were used in their original Latin sense of "longer" and "shorter," and meant simply that some prophets produced longer books than others. Unfortunately, that has given the impression that the church considers some prophets more important than others. It ill behooves us to make such distinctions among the books that constitute God's Word.

In the eighth century B.C., the prophet Micah looked forward to a time when people would "beat their swords into plowshares, and their spears into pruning hooks" (Mic. 4:3). A man who could give the world an ideal like that must never be called "minor." As a matter of fact, the words occur also in one of the "major" prophets. Isaiah has the same vision (cf. 2:4). It is not certain which borrowed from the other, or whether both borrowed from a third. Perhaps it was a kind of floating oracle, the common possession of different regions (Isaiah lived in the capital city of Jerusalem, Micah in the village of Moresheth-Gath, near the Philistine country) and different classes (Isaiah, counselor to kings, apparently belonged to the nobility; Micah, who lived among the farmers and shepherds and rural folk, was supremely the spokesman for the poor).

For all their differences, Isaiah and Micah have identical hopes for the nation and for humankind. A villager in Upper Volta, hearing of United Nations plans for helping his country, said that development "is a whole set of things—living in freedom, justice and health, and working in peace until one is old." It was not otherwise that Micah fashioned humanity's oldest hope: "they shall sit every man under his vine and under his fig tree, and none shall make them afraid" (4:4). Prophetic dreams of the golden age to come regarded it as a time when the entire community should dwell secure, in no fear of war-horses and their chariots, of border raids or slave-hunting expeditions. Families would dwell in unalarmed possession of their houses and fields; young men of draft age would no longer dread receiving notice to leave their quiet pursuits and be inducted into the armed forces. Security from war's alarms would become a reality, accomplished without scrapping the instruments of war but transforming them into the implements of peace; the means of mass destruction transmuted into resources for development; swords beaten into plowshares, spears into pruning hooks.

It is clear from the beginning of Hebrew literature that God's purpose of good toward all humankind embraced a society that knew neither war nor poverty. When, during the Great Depression, the United States first began to take steps to alleviate the plight of the homeless, the hungry, and the unemployed, some who had not been touched by these disasters opposed the use of tax money for the purpose, and thought pastors should support their contention. "After all," they insisted, "Jesus said, 'The poor you will always have with you.' "

They were giving a self-serving twist to what Jesus actually said: "You always have the poor with you" (Mark 14:7). It was not a prediction of the ineradicability of poverty, but a statement of the situation then existing, a statement that has to be understood in context. The shadow of the cross had already begun to lengthen. A woman of imaginative sympathy, a woman whom Jesus had liberated, resolved to do what she could. She could not avert the impending conflict with the powers of the world. She could, however, let him know that she was among those who cared. In an act of self-forgetting devotion, she obtained a cruse of expensive anointing oil and splashed it lavishly upon his body. Some whose shriveled souls had never known the extravagance of love found fault with the deed. "It might have been sold for more than three hundred denarii," they said, almost a year's wage for a laborer, "and the money given to the poor." In happier circumstances, Jesus would no doubt have preferred this, too. But that was not now the alternative, for a devoted follower had spent everything in a gesture of support and goodwill.

Jesus puts the deed in perspective: "you always have the poor with you, and whenever you will, you can do good to them; but you will not always have me. She has done what she could; she has anointed my body beforehand for burying" (Mark 14:7f.), thus giving to her act a significance of which the doer only vaguely dreamed, and assuring her a kind of immortality that the grumblers might have envied: "wherever the gospel is preached in the whole world, what she has done will be told in memory of her" (Mark 14:9).

It is strange that church people more often remember what the complainers said than what the Savior said! If Jesus had affirmed "There will always be poor among you," he would have been faithless to the best ideals of his people. Deuteronomy 15:4f. has it: "There will be no poor among you . . . if only you will obey the voice of the Lord your God, being careful to do all this command-ment which I command you this day." In case the community fails to manage its affairs so as to wipe out poverty, the provision is made that "If there is among you a poor man . . . you shall not harden your heart or shut your hand against your poor brother, but you shall open your hand to him, and lend him sufficient for his need" (Deut. 15:7f.).

Human Mismanagement of God's Bounty

Poverty in any society results from failure to manage God's bounty in such a way that the needs of all may be met. War, too, results from such failure. It was never envisaged that on God's good earth there would be occasion for people to slaughter their brethren. Moses pointed out that maldistribution of goods would lead to violence: "You shall not afflict any widow or orphan. . . . If you do . . . I will kill you with the sword" (Exod. 22:22–24). God's solemn promise was: "If you walk in my statutes and ob-serve my commandments . . . I will give peace in the land . . . and none shall make you afraid; . . . and the sword shall not go through your land" (Lev. 26:3–6).

If our society has poverty, it is time to make such necessary economic arrangements as will obliterate it. John F. Kennedy, at his inauguration, set before the United States two ideals for the 1960s: to put a man on the moon and to wipe out poverty. Though technologically much more difficult, the former was quickly accomplished. As for the latter, nothing much has been accomplished yet. Lyndon Johnson, trying to hold high the torch of his youthful predecessor, declared war on poverty—but many churchpeople, as well as citizens in general, became dropouts.

If our society teeters on the edge of nuclear war, it is time to make such necessary arrangements as will avert the cataclysm. It is important not to overlook the link between poverty and war: they are twins. War impoverishes the earth, and preparation for war impoverishes society. This is clearly happening now in the United States. Every day the world is spending well over $1 billion—*more than $1 billion every day*—in preparation for war. "The money required to provide adequate food, water, education, health and housing for everyone in the world is estimated at $17 billion a year . . . about as much as the world spends on arms every two weeks."[1]

More than half the scientists now alive—physicists, mathematicians, electronics experts—are working to discover and "perfect" more hideous ways of wiping out the human race. For Americans this has already produced calamity. The hand of Mars clutches at higher learning. Institutions that proudly boast of "educating free men without government aid" have given hostages to the god of war. The campus Reserve Officers Training Corps provides some faculty, some student subsidy, and to some extent determines curriculum. Laboratories receive grants and subsidies, not for "pure" research but for "impure" research that seeks out physical and chemical ways of destroying crops, houses, and populations.

Impact, too, is heavy upon state and city governments. Reduction of Medicaid funds threatens nursing-home residents with eviction. Prisons and mental-health institutions go from penury to squalor. Fire and police services are curtailed: between midnight and the morning rush hour, one state now has only six troopers patrolling its entire network of highways. Flight controllers at airports assert that their numbers are too few to handle the current volume of traffic, and computers are inadequately maintained.

Many of America's major cities are bankrupt and continue to function only through fiscal sleight-of-hand. Capital expenditures are deferred and maintenance curtailed, with the result that streets are full of potholes and bridges are in danger of collapse. The vaunted Interstate Highway system has scores of miles of pavement that has crumbled under the weight of ever larger trucks it was not designed to sustain. School lunch programs have been diminished; many school districts have run out of money to pay the teachers and have closed the schools for longer or shorter periods. Some hospitals have closed their doors for lack of funds.

The United States has military bases in almost half a hundred countries; money spent on them increases the deficit in international payments. Between 1960 and 1970 military expenditures abroad accounted for 86.6 percent of the country's $35 billion deficit.[2] Pentagon spending, the largest category of congressional appropriations, like fire, Sheol, and the barren womb, never says "Enough!" (cf. Prov. 30:15f.). Army, navy, and air force provide early retirement, with pensions higher than those of many civilians: an officer who retires at forty can still have a lucrative career in business or government, supplementing high pension with high salary.

The basic problem is that the money the United States spends for armaments makes it impossible for the American economy to function as it ought. The system revolves about two foci: production and consumption. Manufacture of guns, missiles, and bombers short-circuits that system because it creates no consumer goods, provides nothing for the marketplace, nothing that anyone can eat, wear, live in, or ride upon. The bulk of what it produces is either blown up in devastating explosions or else discarded because it became obsolete before it was finished.

Depriving people of consumer goods frustrates the economic system, depreciates the dollar, deprives everyone of security, robs all through merciless inflation. This has given us an existential way of appreciating two biblical allusions. The prophet Haggai (1:6) tells us that in his time "he who earns wages earns wages to put them into a bag with holes." The author of the Apocalypse, picturing inflation in New Testament times, tells of preposterous prices: "A quart of wheat for a denarius" (Rev. 6:6). A denarius was a day's wage for a laborer; after toiling all day, it took everything he had earned to pay for a single quart of wheat!

If Scripture paints our tragic plight, it also points the way out. What we have to do is to "convert" our economy from a war basis to a peace basis, beat our swords into plowshares, our spears into pruning hooks. So far from doing that, we have sometimes conducted intense national campaigns that were the very reverse: turning plowshares into swords and pruning hooks into spears. Anyone old enough to remember World War II will recall how it worked: people tearing down iron railings and steel fences to contribute to the scrap-iron collection. Household items, too, were handed in, from welcome mats to kitchen utensils. Here is the way in which we were invited to participate in grim reversal of the prophetic ideal: one old flatiron, we were told, could be transformed into two steel helmets, and a kitchen sink into twenty-five 3-inch shells. A wash-pail would make three bayonets, and a garbage can one thousand 30-caliber cartridges. A lawn mower was the equivalent of six 3-inch shells, and a set of skid-chains would make twenty 37-mm antiaircraft shells.

America continues to do this. The 96th Congress took $173 million from child welfare funds to pay for two destroyers ordered by the Shah of Iran but not paid for by him. When, at the beginning of the 1980s, there was a determined effort to reduce government expenditure, proposals for cutting the federal budget included no curtailment of military funds but reduction in social security payments, eliminating school lunch programs, dropping the food-stamp program. For some congressmen, said one editor, "the choice is guns or bread—and they choose guns."

Prophetic judgment in the Old Testament came down hard on this reversal of the divine intention. It is, says Joel, because they have despised human rights and the Creator of those rights that doom falls upon Tyre, Sidon, and Philistia. "Prepare war," they say (Joel 3:9f.), in the waging of which the dream of peace is turned upside down: "Beat your plowshares into swords, and your pruning hooks into spears; let the weak say, 'I am a warrior.' "

In such a situation, corruption spreads through all levels of society, and civilians are quick to profit unconscionably from military expenditures. When the United States government announced plans for the race-track railroad system to keep MX missiles in motion, citizens of Nevada rushed to take advantage of the new weaponry destined for their part of the country. Through advance knowledge obtained by a congressman, those "in the know" bought up land that would be used for airport development, a hotel-casino whose business prospects were enormously increased, and territory through which a new highway would pass. Before the new $33 billion missile project had even begun, informed speculators sold for $22,000 an acre land they had acquired at $2,400 an acre. Land they obtained for $3,000 an acre they sold for $62,768 an acre.[3]

Peacemaking: Biblical Imperative and Modern Effort

"Of all the prophets, Micah is perhaps the one whose contribution has been most habitually underestimated," said a biblical commentator.[4] To neglect Micah is to neglect the central thrust of the Old Testament. Peacemaking and peacekeeping are featured in every stratum of the Hebrew–Christian canon. The Old Testament is made up of three parts: the law, the prophets, and the writings. In spite of much that is of a different character, the dream of peace is enshrined in each. Closely associated with Moses the lawgiver was Aaron, his brother. The rabbis regarded Aaron as one who was ever restless in pursuit of peace. "Be of the disciples of Aaron," said Hillel, "loving peace and pursuing it."

"Whoever establishes peace on earth," the rabbis held, "is accounted by Scripture as though he had made it on high." "By three things," they said, "is the world sustained, by justice, by truth, by peace . . . therefore love truth and peace." Nor was it just a private and inner peace they were talking about: "Peace," they held, "embraces all the good in the world, and there is no limit to its benefits."

"By peace," explained the rabbis, "is meant that there should be peace in the world, that there be no wars either between kingdoms or between man and his fellow-men. For just as acts of loving kindness are the pillars of the universe, so is peace—which is expressive of acts of loving kindness. . . . It sustains the world." Psalm 34:14 bids Israel "seek peace, and pursue it." The rabbis interpreted this to mean that the quest for peace was so urgent that all were to pursue it, even if they had to go outside Israel to find it.

It is impressive that the United Nations has reintroduced Micah into American life. On the retaining wall opposite the United Nations buildings in New York, spelled out for all to see, is the prophetic vision: "They shall beat their swords into plowshares and their spears into pruning hooks." What more appropriate inscription to face those who daily work in the Big Glass House, or wend their way to and from meetings of the Security Council, the General Assembly, the Economic and Social Council, or committees concerned with the peace and security of the world?

That is not all. On the grounds of the United Nations, in the North Garden, there is a heroic-sized statue of a big-muscled man with an enormous sledgehammer actually beating and bending swords into plowshares. Micah's vision of a warless world is humankind's oldest dream. What is new in the world is this organization, now with more than 150 states banded together by the United Nations Charter "to save succeeding generations from the scourge of war."

In 1979 the United Nations held a special session on disarmament. For many, it was a disappointment that Jimmy Carter, who had begun his presidency by affirming his intention "to strengthen the entire United Nations system," chose not to attend. There was, however, overwhelming evidence that for most people on our planet the dream of peace has become a matter of utmost urgency. There was presented, for example, a Japanese petition with 20 million signatures, pleading for complete nuclear disarmament and outlawing as a crime against humanity the use of nuclear weapons.

At Princeton, New Jersey, there was held during the same summer the Third Assembly of the World Conference on Peace and Religion, with 338 representatives from forty-seven countries. All the major religions were represented in the attendance: Buddhism, Christianity, Confucianism, Hinduism, Jainism, Judaism, Islam, Shinto, Sikhism, Zoroastrianism, and others. Deploring the fact that religion is now too often thought of as a department of human activity largely devoted to private piety, the group went on record as opposing the arms race with its threat of war and annihilation. Thomas à Kempis long ago observed that "All men desire peace, but few desire the things that make for peace."

A poll of Roman Catholics in West Germany disclosed that the greatest concern was for "a chance to live without war." Seventy percent felt that the most urgent task of the churches was to remind the world's statesmen and stateswomen of their obligation to do justice and promote peace. Norman Thomas left the Presbyterian ministry because "the church always says the right thing—too late." In 1979 Richard Watts, a Presbyterian pastor in Cleveland, Ohio, resigned his charge in order to establish a "Swords into Plowshares" program for the churches in the Western Reserve area of Ohio. The Southern Baptist church held an unprecedented convocation on disarmament. Letters now sent from the Riverside Church in New York City carry the slogan "Reverse the Arms Race."

What is true in Germany, Japan, and the United States appears to be true of the common people in all parts of the world. Many who view the United Nations statue of the mighty man beating swords into plowshares are surprised to discover the sculptor's name: Eugeniv Vuchetich. The sculpture is a duplicate of one that stands at the entrance to the Tretyakov Art Gallery in Moscow. The one in New York was presented to the United Nations by Nikita Kruschchev when, in 1959, he introduced into the United Nations General Assembly a resolution calling for general and complete disarmament, an appeal never taken seriously by the United States.

The statue reveals something about the common people of Russia that must not be forgotten. Christianity was very early introduced into the land. By the fourth century there were churches along the Black Sea. Around A.D. 1000, Vladimir, grand duke of Kiev—who became St. Vladimir—was converted, made Greek Orthodoxy the official religion, and devoted the rest of his life to the erection of churches, schools, and libraries. If Christianity in Russia has suffered persecution on account of its indifference to the common life, this statue is state-sponsored reassurance that atheism has not suppressed Micah's dream.

The first pope ever to visit the United States came in the hope of making peace. Paul VI flew from Rome one night, carried out a crowded schedule in New York, and returned to the Vatican the next night. In his address to the United Nations he spoke of "sound ways of peace." At the nearby Holy Family Church, he said: "The work of peace is not restricted to one religious belief; it is the work and duty of every human person, regardless of religious convictions. Men are brothers, God is their Father, and their Father wills that they live in peace with one another as brothers should." Pope John Paul II, who visited the United Nations in 1979, quoted the words of Paul VI: "No more war. War never again," and added his own concern to destroy "the very roots of hatred, destructiveness, and contempt . . . in the systems that decide the history of all our societies." So vast are the stockpiles of weapons that Pope John Paul II pointed to the imminent danger that "sometime, somewhere, somehow, someone can set in motion the terrible mechanism of general destruction."

"Peace," Adlai Stevenson once said, "is the unfinished business of mankind." The papal visits to the United Nations served to put this unfinished business in perspective. The distinction between the concerns of religion and politics, church and government seemed to disappear. Diplomats were heartened to discern that churchpeople were supporting their endeavors. Churchpeople came to see that peacemaking has to do with such mundane matters as the care and feeding of refugees, the use of insecticides to destroy mosquitoes before they destroy people, the building of dams that transform rushing torrents into electric currents.

The whole world's problem was summed up by General Dwight D. Eisenhower: "Every gun made, every warship launched, every rocket fired, signifies a theft from those who hunger and are not fed, those who are cold and are not clothed." It is sometimes argued that we cannot afford to follow the prophet's vision, because turning swords into plowshares would put people out of work. J. B. Priestley tells of an English miner who, in the days before 1914, could find no work. The war came and the government sent him into the army. "Society," the miner observed, "has no work for me except when there is killing to be done." Can this be the kind of social order God wills for the world? Can Christians look with indifference and unconcern upon a system that does that to its people?

We are not yet organized to plan for peace. When a bill calling for the conversion of armaments into civilian goods was introduced into the United States Congress, there was not even a committee to which it could be referred. The 1967 Confession of Faith commits the United Presbyterian church to the belief that "the

church, in its own life, is called to practice the forgiveness of enemies and to commend to the nations as practical politics the
search for co-operation and peace." Certainly the determination
to outdistance all others in the arms race has not proved to be
practical politics.

In a 1953 address to the United Nations, President Eisenhower
said: "Let no one think that the expenditure of vast sums for
weapons and systems of defense can guarantee absolute safety for
the cities and citizens of any nation. The awful arithmetic of the
atomic bomb does not permit of any such easy solution." In 1956
the general-turned-president went even further. "The era of security through armaments," he said, "has ended and the human
race must conform its action to this truth or die." Robert McNa-
mara, onetime United States secretary of defense, has expressed a
similar judgment: "Excessive military spending," he said, "can
erode security rather than enhance it."

When those who know the most about the military warn us not
to trust it, it is time for the church to press the case for converting
swords and spears into tools of production. Some experiments
along that line demonstrate how practical it can be. In 1969 the
United States government closed Brookley Air Force base in
Mobile, Alabama. The loss of 13,600 civilian jobs brought bitter-
ness to the citizens of Mobile. Ten years later, they had come to
regard it as the best thing that ever happened to their community.
In leaving, the Pentagon abandoned several thousand acres of
land with streets and water and sewer lines already in place. The
vast property, only ten minutes from downtown, had a 10,000-
foot frontage on Mobile Bay.

All this, readily converted to civilian use, quickly became a
bustling subcity. The runways and aviation buildings became a
general airport. A 392-acre area was turned into an industrial
park. In one enormous hangar, International Systems, Inc.,
found it feasible to manufacture concrete modular housing units
for shipment abroad. Another 24 acres became a city park, and
289 acres and their buildings were transformed into a new campus
for the University of South Alabama. There were other happy
surprises. The federal government pays no taxes; the new busi-
nesses provided much needed revenue for the city. Private in-
dustry had avoided the area because it did not wish to compete

with the salaries and other benefits provided to government workers. Lieutenant-General Walter K. Wilson, Jr., retired chief of the Army Corps of Engineers, headed the civilian committee searching for ways to convert the property to peaceful purposes. "In my opinion," he said, "we are a lot better off now."

When Boeing-Vertol, near Philadelphia, Pennsylvania, lost out in competition for manufacturing military helicopters for the 1980s, it did not lay off its workers, but set them to producing what America badly needs: "a fleet of quiet, fast, comfortable railway cars and electric trolleys." Within a comparatively short time, there had been notable improvement in the public transportation systems of Boston, San Francisco, and Chicago. The army has for some time been threatening to dismantle Fort Dix. Plans have been repeatedly deferred because of dismay at the thought of civilian jobs that would be lost. Some take a different view. They would convert the vast area into a badly needed airport to serve metropolitan New Jersey and New York. One pilot points out that it could become "a major point of exchange in the flow of people and goods between North America, Europe, Africa, and South America."

Labor unions, too, are now lining up on the side of Micah. William Winpisinger, president of the Machinists' Union and the man whom Senator George McGovern called "the American trade union movement's ambassador to the future," has become co-chairman of SANE, an organization for action on disarmament and the peace race. Hitherto, organized labor has opposed disarmament on the ground that it deprived labor of jobs. A study entitled "The Impact of Military Spending on the Machinists' Union" changed the mind of the union president. He now proclaims that conversion to a peacetime economy is an idea whose time has come, and identifies conversion as "a basic self-interest of workers."

"We reached the point long ago," says Winpisinger, "where we were no longer enamored of the virtues of defense employment. Military spending is wasteful. The defense budget of this country is inflationary—flat out. We can cut it immediately."[5] Disarmament provides more jobs than armament. Two B-1 bombers cost $204 million. For that sum Americans could build 11,000 low-cost homes and give work to 20,000 unemployed; operate twelve

600-pupil middle schools for thirty-five years and thereby create 37,200 jobs; operate 70 neighborhood clinics for thirty years and thereby create 27,800 jobs.

The prophets were nothing if not practical. To his vision of converting weapons into tools, Micah adds: "Nation shall not lift up sword against nation, neither shall they learn war any more" (4:3). Our society has many ways of teaching us war: a military academy, a coastguard academy, a naval academy, an air force academy—but not a peace academy. In public schools, history is too much taught in terms of wars and battles and military heroes, not enough in terms of thinkers and teachers and inventors. Childhood games are too often built around playing at war, with guns and tanks and battleships among one's earliest toys. Theological seminaries spend more time in teaching students to operate audio-visual machines than in cultivating the arts of peace.

Across the street from United Nations headquarters, American church communions have built the Church Center for the United Nations, containing a chapel of striking design; on the altar are the words of Jesus: "Would that you knew the things that belong to peace." Within the United Nations complex itself there is no "church" as such; however, there is a small meditation chapel, always open, and open to delegates from every nation, whatever their religious community may be. The very structure of the room powerfully portrays in yet another way Micah's ideal.

In the great 38-story secretariat building there was felt the need for something that would give the feeling of weight, solidity, permanence. The massive "altar" in the meditation room is a huge block of iron ore, upon which shines a shaft of light—much as, in a presentation of Bach's *St. Matthew Passion*, no human figure represented Jesus: he was, instead, symbolized by a column of golden light streaming from above. In the great house devoted to turning swords into plowshares there is this huge mass of raw iron, of which the designer said that it "represents the very paradox of human life; the basic material offered to us by God may be used either for construction or for destruction."

At the dedication of this meditation room, Dag Hammarskjöld, then United Nations secretary-general, said:

We want to bring back in this room the stillness which we have lost in the streets and in our conference rooms. . . . We want to bring back our thoughts to great and simple truths, to the way in which the light of the skies gives life to the earth on which we stand—a symbol . . . of what the spirit gives to man. We want to bring back the life of worship, devotion to something which is greater and higher than ourselves. We want [by the form of the altar] to bring to everybody's mind the fact that every single one of us is faced, in the handling of the riches of this earth, with the choice between the plowshare and the sword.

Russell Baker reports New England bumper stickers reading "Think Bluefish" and "Think Tennis." God's people need bumper stickers of more sober wording: "Think Peace!" or "Ore is for tilling, not for killing!" Thus the prophet's dream will become real and the nations themselves will be presented as a worthy offering to the God of Peace.

8

The Offering Up
of Nations

After David brought the ark to the capital city, Judaism had one central shrine, and there the temple was built. After the destruction of Jerusalem, it was the widely scattered synagogue that enabled Judaism to survive. There could be a synagogue in any place where there were as many as ten heads of families willing to take responsibility for it. There were synagogues in Egypt, Asia, and Europe. As the Hebrews prepared to return from exile, their thoughts turned again to worship at one focal point—except that now it was to be not for Jews alone. The prophet Isaiah heard God say, ". . . my house shall be called a house of prayer for all peoples" (56:7).

It was to Jerusalem that Diaspora Jews brought their offerings at appropriate times. Isaiah pictured a new kind of offering. From lands wide-scattered, the survivors "shall bring all your brethren from all the nations as an offering to the Lord, . . . all flesh shall come to worship before me, says the Lord." Every known mode of travel will be used to bring about this happy assembly: they shall come "upon horses, and in chariots, and in litters, and upon mules, and upon dromedaries, to my holy mountain" (66:20, 23).

The early Christians thought of themselves not as gathered *from* the nations, but as distributed *among* the nations so as to infiltrate everywhere. Early in the second century an unknown writer made this observation:

102

The Christians are not distinguished from other men by country, by language, nor by civil institutions. For they neither dwell in cities by themselves, nor use a peculiar tongue, nor lead a singular mode of life. They dwell in the Grecian or barbarian cities, as the case may be; they follow the usage of the country in dress, food, and the other affairs of life. Yet they present a wonderful and confessedly paradoxical conduct.

They dwell in their own native lands, but as strangers. They take part in all things, as citizens; and they suffer all things, as foreigners. Every foreign country is a fatherland to them, and every native land is foreign. They marry, like all others; they have children; but they do not cast away their offspring. They have the table in common, but not wives. They are in the flesh, but do not live after the flesh. They obey the existing laws, and excel the laws by their lives. They love all, and are persecuted by all. . . . They are poor and make many rich. They lack all things, and in all things abound. . . . By the Jews they are attacked as aliens, and by the Greeks persecuted; and the cause of the enmity their enemies cannot tell. In short, what the soul is in the body, the Christians are in the world.[1]

The early church took seriously Jesus' teaching and example concerning peace, and practiced his tactic of overcoming evil with good. Its members did not fight for their rights, nor for their country. Kenneth Scott Latourette says that "for the first three centuries no Christian writing which has survived to our time condoned Christian participation in war."[2] Hippolytus (born ca. A.D. 217) set down what he believed to be the apostolic tradition on this subject. He maintained that when a soldier applied for admission to the church he must agree that he would not kill, even if commanded to do so by his superiors. Military commanders who wished to become Christians must resign their commissions. A baptized person who wished to enlist in the army must be cut off from the church.

Toward the end of the second century, Tertullian (who lived ca. A.D. 160–230) declared that in bidding Peter put up his sword Christ had disarmed every soldier. Born in Carthage, son of a military commander serving in a Roman legion assigned to North Africa, Tertullian argued that Christians could not join the Roman army because this would mean swearing allegiance to the emperor. In affirming that "Jesus is Lord," the New Testament declares that Caesar is not Lord and that the Christian can serve only one Master.

Tertullian held, nevertheless, that by exemplifying a larger loyalty, the Christians were doing far more for the emperor than the pagans were. Origen (ca. A.D. 185–254), a North African Christian from Alexandria, contended that Christians, in rejecting military service, were better citizens of the empire than if they had accepted it, since by their prayers they "vanquish all demons who stir up war and disturb the peace."

The "Just War" Doctrine

Starting with the fourth century, things became different. In A.D. 312 Emperor Constantine not only embraced Christianity, thereby declaring it no longer illegal, but placed it on a par with other religions of his domain. Constantine's emblem became not a cross but a spear overlaid with gold, a transverse bar forming a semblance of the cross. Allegiance to the state, carrying with it military obligation, was now deemed to surmount all other loyalties—and when the empire in due course was breaking up, Christians were accused of undermining it: their ethics had made it difficult to deal with the barbarians!

To this charge of undermining, Augustine replied with his *City of God*; he (and others) developed the doctrine of the "just war." A war is "just" only if it is fought by a legitimate authority (not by a guerrilla band) against a recognized evil. It must not be undertaken against foolish odds, but must have a reasonable chance of success. It must be fought without unnecessary violence, and it must be waged for the establishment of peace. Moreover, it has to be fought with inward love!

Thus the church has had to live with the doctrine of the just war, but rulers have usually managed to persuade themselves that any and every proposed war fully conformed to those requirements. In the "just war" concept, the clergy and all in monastic orders were to be exempt. Thus draft deferment for ministers was the rule until some of them in the twentieth century declined to accept preferred status, insisting that their unwillingness to participate in war should be dealt with in the same way as that of any other conscientious objector.

The medieval church also urged upon society as a whole what was called the "peace of God." The letter to the Philippians speaks in one breath about "the peace of God" (4:7) and in the next about "the God of peace" (4:9). During the Middle Ages, the term "peace of God" was used in a very limited sense, to describe something far less than is wished for by the God of peace. Although the Roman church succeeded to the power and prestige of the Roman empire, it was not able to maintain the Pax Romana. The feudal barons jealously guarded their right to wage private wars.

One writer describes the resulting situation: "Every hill was a stronghold, every plain a battlefield. The trader was robbed on the highway, the peasant was killed at his plow, the priest was slain at the altar. Neighbor fought against neighbor, baron against baron, city against city."[3] In its call to the Crusades, the church sought to sublimate this bellicose spirit. It was not a very far cry from that to a holy war.

Bernard of Clairvaux, preaching the Second Crusade, made this appeal: "Christian warriors, He who gave His life for you, today demands yours in return. These are combats worthy of you, combats in which it is glorious to conquer and advantageous to die. Illustrious knights, generous defenders of the Cross, remember the example of your fathers, who conquered Jerusalem, and whose names are inscribed in heaven. Abandon then the things that perish, to gather unfading palms, and to conquer a kingdom that has no end."

Crusades were waged not only to recover the "holy places," but also against the Cathari sect and other groups whom the pope deemed heretical. The papacy endorsed the long series of Crusades: armies of Western Europe moved eastward under the cry, "God wills it!" Crusaders bent on recovering the "tomb of Christ" had apparently never read the Gospels: "He is not here! He is risen!"

If the church sought to capitalize on the military spirit of the feudal era to recruit men for the Crusades, it tried at home to keep its members from fighting each other. Thus in France, in the early part of the eleventh century, there was an effort to abolish warfare between Christians. The church proclaimed what it called the Peace of God. In the name of the God of peace it commanded all people to refrain not only from war but also from robbery and violence of every kind. If there were to be fighting, it must be within certain bounds: "There should be no attacks on the buildings of the Church, nor upon clergymen, pilgrims, merchants, women and farmers; and cattle and farming tools should be spared."[4]

In the year 1023 a French bishop proposed that feudal nobles subscribe to this oath:

> I will not take away ox nor cow nor any other beast of burden. I will not seize the peasant nor the peasant's wife nor the merchants. I will not take away their money, nor will I force them to ransom themselves. I do not want them to lose their property through a war that their lord wages, and I will not whip them to get their nourishment away from them. From the first of March to All Saints' Day I will seize neither horse nor mare nor colt from the pasture. I will not destroy and burn houses; I will not uproot and devastate vineyards under pretext of war; I will not destroy mills nor steal their flour.

Here is war by the calendar! From the first of March to All Saints' Day is the larger part of the year. Nevertheless, that eight months' period still left four months during which certain types of plunder were not under the ban. The difficulties encountered by this open-season, closed-season on war suggested that it might be more practical to forget the Peace of God and concentrate upon something called the Truce of God.

Under the influence of the Cluniac revival, the bishops in A.D. 1041 issued an edict requiring communicants to maintain a holy and unbroken peace during certain days of the week and certain seasons of the Christian year. From Thursday evening of each week to the following Monday morning—the days considered peculiarly holy because associated with Jesus' death and resurrection—everybody was expected to observe what an even more violent age has come to call a "cease-fire." This was extended also to certain ecclesiastical holidays, and anyone who violated the terms was threatened with excommunication. All the countries of Western Europe were eventually committed to this attempt to make life more tolerable on weekends.

Insofar as the Truce of God had any effect, it was largely to serve the cause of greater violence. The measure of security that it won for the ruling classes enabled the barons and feudal knights to leave their properties under the protection of the church while they responded to its call for war against the Muslims. In the seventh century, Jerusalem had fallen to the fanatical exponents of a faith that its devotees held to be an extension and intensification of Israel's faith. Almost immediately the papacy began scheming to recover the "holy places." Not for one week but for several hundred years the church sought to harness all its energies for this purpose. The Crusades may indeed be thought of as the foreign policy of the papacy. They produced such romantic figures as Peter the Hermit, Raymond of Toulouse, and Richard the Lion-Hearted. The so-called Christian Kingdom of Jerusalem lasted from 1131 to 1489.

Psalm 106 describes how God sometimes gives his people what they want materially, but with it sends leanness of soul. This is what happened while the church was attempting to sanctify the martial spirit. Warriors marching under the banner of the cross did eventually recover—if but temporarily—the so-called holy places. Yet the church also got other things for which it had not bargained. Urban II, proclaiming the First Crusade, explained that "the papacy desires a perfect and universal church, and a perfect and universal church must reign in the Holy Land." The somewhat imperfect results of this non sequitur have remained to curse both the church and the world. Urban wished to restore unity between East and West. Instead, he shattered it, for the Crusades destroyed the Byzantine empire and Constantinople fell to the Turks. Christendom's greatest church, Hagia Sophia, became a mosque and Orthodox culture and influence declined. Throughout the East, the Crusades created a bad image of Christianity. When the papal warriors took Jerusalem, the blood of the conquered ran down the streets until the conquerors splashed in it as they rode. The victors entered the "Holy Sepulchre" and folded their bloodstained hands in prayer.

In any case, the Crusaders did not succeed in permanently restoring to the West sovereignty over Near Eastern sites. They did leave among Muslims the impression, strong to this day, that Christianity is a warlike religion. From this era, too, dates that hostility to Jews that has so long been a curse of Christendom. The Crusades, says Latourette, "were an aspect of the partial capture of the Church by the warrior tradition and habits of the barbarian peoples who had mastered Western Europe and had given their professed allegiance to the Christian faith."[5] Medieval Europe based its hope for world order on the achievement of a universal state with two heads, the pope and the Holy Roman emperor. It is clear that the God of Peace wishes for his world a peace that is different from that for which the church-state wages war.

The Nations of the World—A Living Sacrifice

The Roman empire was covered with a network of roads, over which troops could move with surprising rapidity. The earliest Christians traveled those roads proclaiming "the gospel of peace" (Eph. 6:15). Inevitably as they went, they thought of Christ as Lord of a still vaster domain. Paul is always dreaming of "lands beyond" (2 Cor. 10:16), and closes the letter to the Romans with the hope of stopping by to see them as he makes his way to Spain (cf. 15:28), farthest spot on the map of the known world. He must do this because Christ "came and preached peace to you who were far off and peace to those who were near" (Eph. 2:17).

Paul says, indeed, that as a minister of Christ he is in "the priestly service of the gospel of God, so that the offering of the Gentiles may be accceptable, sanctified by the Holy Spirit" (Rom. 15:16). He has in mind that high point of Old Testament religion, Isaiah's vision of Israel, itself redeemed from bondage, bringing "all your brethren from all the nations as an offering to the Lord" (Isa. 66:20). The whole purpose of Paul's incessant itineration was to place the nations upon the altar as an offering to the God of the whole creation.

Here is universalization of the Old Testament system of ceremonial worship. Primitive peoples believed that sacrifices burnt upon an altar had power to establish rapport between human beings and God. The sacrifice was sometimes thought of as a meal in which both human and God participated. Sometimes the emphasis was upon the smoke, which mysteriously ascended on high and pleased the nostrils of the deity. Paul's figure of speech brings before us the whole picture of altar, priest, and sacrifice. Paul is the priest, his apostolate a transmuted priesthood in which his priestly service is to offer up the oblations that are due.

What Paul places upon the altar, however, is not bulls or goats, pigeons or turtledoves. He offers upon the altar the nations. The people of all lands are the oblation, not to be consumed by fire but to be a "living sacrifice, holy and acceptable to God" (Rom. 12:1). The letter to the Hebrews expresses the same thought in a slightly different way. Christ is himself both priest and sacrifice: ". . . we have been sanctified through the offering of the body of Jesus Christ once for all. . . . By a single offering he has perfected for all time those who are sanctified" (Heb. 10:10, 14).

What Christ placed upon the altar was his body. His body is the church: "And for their sake I consecrate myself, that they also may be consecrated in truth." "As thou didst send me into the world, so I have sent them into the world" (John 17:19, 18). The highest levels of New Testament thought proclaim that the church as both the body of Christ and the servant of Christ has as its supreme duty the presentation of all nations upon the altar of the living God, the God who desires not sacrifice but justice and mercy (cf. Matt. 23:23).

It is impressive in this connection that so much of biblical terminology has been adapted to the one universal agency now uniting all nations in pursuit of peace. Article 7 of the United Nations Charter establishes as "the principal organs of the United Nations: A General Assembly, a Security Council, an Economic and Social Council, a Trusteeship Council, an International Court of Justice. . . ." The very terms by which these organs are designated are strangely familiar to those conversant with the nomenclature of religion concerned with world redemption.

"Assembly" is a term anciently used by polytheistic people for a plenary session of the pantheon. The Greeks originally believed that gods lived on Mount Olympus, hidden by a wall of clouds. In the later poets, however, the real abode of the gods was in the vault of the sky: they gathered on Olympus for solemn assembly. In the ancient Near East also there was belief in "the mount of assembly in the far north" (Isa. 14:13), where the gods met and the deities of the Ugaritic myths held conclave. One of the Hebrew terms for "congregation," derived from the verb "to appoint," designates a company assembled by appointment.

"General Assembly" is a phrase from the King James Version of the Bible, where reference is made (Heb. 12:23) to a "general assembly" held on Mount Zion. Judges 20:1f. (NEB) tells how "All the Israelites, the whole community from Dan to Beersheba . . . left their homes as one man and assembled before the Lord at Mizpah. The leaders of the people and all the tribes of Israel presented themselves in the general assembly of the people of God." Since the ancients represented the gods in assembly on mountains, a gathering of top diplomatic officials is now referred to as a "meeting at the summit," and the coming together of people from all lands is a "general assembly."

The Security Council of the United Nations has primary responsibility "to maintain or restore international peace and security." The Hebrew-Christian Scriptures regularly link peace and security. King Hezekiah thought, "There will be peace and security in my days" (Isa. 39:8; cf. 2 Kings 20:19). The prophet Ezekiel looked forward to a time when his people should "dwell securely, and none shall make them afraid" (34:28). To laggards rejecting their responsibility as members of a community, Paul wrote: "When people say, 'There is peace and security,' then sudden destruction will come upon them as travail comes upon a woman with child" (1 Thess. 5:3).

The Economic and Social Council of the United Nations has responsibility for initiating "studies and reports with respect to international economic, social, cultural, educational, health, and related matters" and making "recommendations for the purpose of promoting respect for, and observance of, human rights and fundamental freedoms for all." These have been the practical concerns of high religion in every age and place. It could be shown how each is deeply rooted in Scripture.

The Trusteeship Council of the United Nations is charged with bringing to self-government those territories "held under mandate," "detached from enemy states," or "voluntarily placed under the system." Trusteeship is familiar to students of religion. The New Testament speaks of how humanity has undergone a period of tutelage "under guardians and trustees" (Gal. 4:2). The word translated "trustees" describes the legal guardian who looks after the property of minors until they come of age. It is the same word that, in English, has become "economist," literally a manager of household accounts, a steward, one occupying a position of trust. Religion does not find it strange that the United Nations Trusteeship Council is concerned "to ensure equal treatment in social, economic and commercial matters."

The International Court of Justice is "the principal judicial organ of the United Nations." To it member states may appeal for settlement of legal disputes; to it nonmember states, under certain circumstances, may also appeal; from it the other organs of the United Nations may seek advisory opinions. Justice and the impartial administration of justice are high on the agenda of every religion. A petition in the Book of Common Prayer reads: "Grant us grace . . . to make no peace with oppression; and, that we may reverently use our freedom, help us to employ it in the maintenance of justice among men and nations."

Jesus' parable of the Great Assize, in Matthew 25:31ff., pictures a court of international justice at work. An often overlooked aspect of the scene is that the court is in session for the trial, not of individuals, but of nations. Before the Judge of all the earth are to be "gathered all the nations." It is impressive, too, that adjudication is given with respect to matters about which the United Nations is concerned: "I was naked and you clothed me, I was sick and you visited me, I was in prison and you came to me." This is linked with another responsibility, which especially at this time in the world's life seems to belong to the nations: "I was hungry and you gave me food, I was thirsty and you gave me drink, I was a stranger and you welcomed me."

Feeding God's People

In the intricate structure of the twentieth century's industrialized life, provision for the hungry must be made on a scale such as only nations can manage. The guarantee of an adequate water supply may involve agreement regarding rivers that pay no attention to national boundaries. The welcoming of strangers may necessitate revision of immigration policies and reception of untold numbers of refugees.

At this writing there are many lands that ravaging hunger makes desolate. Somalia, with an annual per-capita income of $125, has had its population of 4 million augmented by a million Ethiopian refugees, many already suffering from malnutrition frequently exacerbated by malaria or dysentery. Drought and human mismanagement have induced famine in the Karamoja region of Uganda; planting has been disrupted by war. Lands just south of the Sahara Desert—including Chad and Mauritania—have for years faced a major shortage of food due to inadequate rainfall. To provide its people with a subsistence diet, Mauritania annually requires 180,000 tons of cereals, but is able to produce only 28,000 tons. In order to survive a little while longer in Kampuchea, people have been eating the rice intended to be used for seed.

The unequal distribution of food in today's world was dramatized at a meeting of the United Presbyterian General Assembly. As the delegates arrived one morning, each drew at random a colored card assigning him or her, not by any right or merit of the person's own, "but simply by the luck of the draw," to one of five areas representing the continents. Not until later did participants become aware that tables outside their own area differed from their own.

Tables in the "Africa" section were bare, those in "Asia" had placemats. In the "Latin America" section, there were placemats or tablecloths made of old newspapers. "Europe" offered proper tablecloths, napkins, plates, plastic cutlery, cups for coffee, and small containers of orange juice. "North America" had the juice and coffee on tables that were lavishly set: linen, silver, china, candles, crystal, flowers.

For the first three-quarters of an hour, no one ate. Attention was focused instead upon "the inequitable distribution of resources among the world's people—areas with the greatest numbers and need having the smallest resources, those with the smaller numbers having the greatest." A five-foot loaf of bread, symbolizing the world's total protein consumption, was brought forward; representatives of the five continents were invited to receive portions. Five percent went to the Asian representative, 10 percent to the African, 15 percent to the Latin American, 25 percent to the European, 45 percent to the North American. These portions had to be broken up for distribution to the disproportionate numbers in each area.

Finally, it was time for breakfast. Asians, Africans, and Latin Americans were told to move to the serving table and provide for themselves as directed: Asians could take coffee and roll; Africans could have juice, coffee, and roll; Latin Americans could have juice, coffee, roll, and eggs. Things were different at the European and North American tables, where everyone remained seated and was formally served by liveried waiters. Europeans received full breakfasts: juice, coffee, rolls, eggs, and three big sausages. North Americans had the same and, in addition, they were served Danish rolls and were offered seconds or as much as they wanted of everything.

It soon dawned on those in the last two areas that they should share their bounty. Accordingly, they were soon sending their surplus into the areas where only a token meal had been provided. The result was that there was enough to go around. Everybody ate—and was satisfied. At almost the same time a gourmet food editor was reporting in a magazine on a restaurant he had visited in an eastern city where, although he was careful to choose the least expensive wines, dinner for two came to $196.50.

Nothing is more characteristic of the ministry of Jesus than concern that the hungry should be fed. He taught his disciples to pray, not for blue-chip stocks, not for gourmet food, not for pie in the sky, but for daily bread: the Greek word means the journeyman laborer's wage, paid to him at the end of the day, to tide him over the next day's need. Contemporary translations now read: "Give us today our bread for the morrow" (M; RSV mg.; NEB mg.). Hardly anything in the Gospels is so well documented as Jesus' insistence that everybody should have daily bread.

When he had restored to health a young girl thought to have been at the point of death, and everyone stood around doing nothing because they were "overcome with amazement," Jesus was the one who remembered that she might be hungry. It was he who said: "Give her something to eat" (Mark 5:42–43). Adults, too, get hungry—even strong men in the prime of life. Jesus was not indifferent to that. When the disciples, going through the grain fields on the Sabbath, felt an emptiness in their stomachs, they "began to pluck ears of grain" to eat (Mark 2:23). This kind of living on the countryside was permitted to Hebrew travelers. They were not expected to use a sickle, but it was perfectly legal to gather what they could with their hands.

Since it was the Sabbath, the pious began to quibble. This was harvesting, and Sabbath harvesting was not allowed. Human hunger was entitled to no consideration when it involved a legalism like this. Jesus not only applauded what the disciples had done, but to the critics cited the example of David, Israel's best-loved king, who, when he was hungry, even ate the Bread of the Presence, reverently kept on display by the priests (cf. Matt. 12:1ff.). Moreover, Jesus used this incident to reiterate one of the foremost ideals of high religion, and to make clear how he had come to fulfill it: "And if you had known what this means, 'I desire mercy, and not sacrifice,' you would not have condemned the guiltless. For the Son of man is lord of the sabbath" (Matt. 12:7–8).

Children get hungry, adults get hungry—and crowds get hungry. Mark tells of an occasion when the Galileans were thronging Jesus so that he and his companions "had no leisure even to eat" (6:31). By going to the other side of the lake, he hoped for respite, but when he landed he found they had got there ahead of him. So far from reacting angrily, "he had compassion on them . . . and he began to teach them many things." By this time it was growing late, and the disciples said to him: "This is a lonely place, and the hour is now late; send them away. . . [to] buy themselves something to eat." Jesus answered: "You give them something to eat" (6:34–37).

There follows the feeding of the multitude, specifically the feeding of five thousand. There is in the Gospels the story of still another feeding of a multitude, this time four thousand. These incidents are related more fully than most incidents in the ministry of Jesus. The feeding of the five thousand is the one "miracle" related in all four Gospels. In addition, Mark and Matthew tell of the feeding of four thousand. Altogether there are at least eight

Gospel narratives setting forth Jesus' insistence that when people are hungry they should be fed.

Artists have been fond of painting Jesus breaking bread with human beings: feeding the multitudes on the hillside; at supper with his disciples; making himself known to unnamed friends in Emmaus. This aspect of the incarnation is one of the ways in which Jesus fulfilled the prophets. Feeding the hungry was a significant part of the ministries of both Elijah and Elisha. It was precisely Jesus' concern for the hungry that demonstrated how completely he fulfilled Hebrew expectations as to what the Messiah would do.

This concern that people should be fed was also a factor in the people's attributing to him the qualities of deity. Psalm 145:15f. praises the Creator's sustaining care: "The eyes of all look to thee, and thou givest them their food in due season. Thou openest thy hand, thou satisfiest the desire of every living thing." During the wilderness wanderings, God sustained his people with manna, called by the psalmist "the grain of heaven . . . the bread of the angels" (78:24f.).

It was in such terms that Jesus described the gift of himself to humanity: "the living bread which came down from heaven" (John 6:51). Plainly, a church which daily prays, "Give us today our bread for the morrow" must also implement the Lord's command, "Give them something to eat." Periodic fasting, or missing an occasional lunch, or filling penny-a-meal mite boxes will not do it. It requires exercise of citizenship to influence public policy, and enthusiastic support of the United Nations Food and Agriculture Organization.

In Jesus' parable those praised for having met their obligations were hardly aware that they had done it. Their immediate concern had been to manage resources so as to meet needs at hand—and their bounty had reached beyond their imagining. On the other hand, no charge of piracy or genocide is brought against those who are rejected. They are turned away, not because they have sent people to concentration camps or popped them into ovens. All that happened was that they did not give food to the hungry, water to the thirsty, clothing to the naked, shelter to the homeless.

These people, too, are surprised at the verdict. "When?" they asked. They were unaware of failure to provide for the needy.

Their crime was that they did not know there were any needy. Intent on building up the Gross National Product, they had not noticed the hungry, the sick, the dispossessed. The United Nations exists not simply to "save succeeding generations from the scourge of war" but also in order to "establish conditions under which justice . . . can be maintained." The church exists to make sure that agglomerations of people do not overlook or neglect the elemental obligations of members of the human family, and that nations, so far from being cast onto history's dungheap, may be presented as "a fragrant offering, an acceptable sacrifice, pleasing to God" (Phil. 4:18, NEB).

Notes

1: Yahweh Is a Man of War

1. Senator John Culver, then a member of the U.S. Senate Armed Services Committee, quoted in the public press.
2. George A. Buttrick and Keith R. Crim, eds., *Interpreter's Dictionary of the Bible*, 5 vols. (Nashville: Abingdon, 1976), 2:656.
3. George Adam Smith, *The Book of the Twelve Prophets*, 2 vols. (New York: George H. Doran Co., n.d.), 1:425, 424.
4. *Book of the Twelve Prophets*, 2:136.
5. Ibid., p. 144.

2: Not by Military Might

1. *Interpreter's Dictionary of the Bible*, 3:260.
2. Herodotus, *History* 2:141.
3. George A. Buttrick et al., eds., *The Interpreter's Bible*, 12 vols. (Nashville: Abingdon, 1952–57), 2:580.
4. George A. Buttrick and Keith R. Crim, eds., *Interpreter's Dictionary of the Bible*, 5 vols. (Nashville: Abingdon, 1976), 2:836.
5. Buttrick et al., *The Interpreter's Bible* 2:582.

3: Prophet to the Nations

1. Josephus, *Antiquities* 18.3.1.
2. Ibid., 18.3.1f.
3. *Legatio ad Gaium xxxviii.*

4: Prince of Peace

1. Major, Manson, and Wright, *The Mission and Message of Jesus* (New York: Dutton, 1938), p. 412.
2. John Skinner, *Prophecy and Religion* (Cambridge, Eng.: Cambridge University Press, 1926), p. 210; cf. chap. 11 in its entirety.

3. Peter Bassell, in *New York Times Book Review*, May 23, 1976, p. 8.

4. Harrison E. Salisbury, *War between Russia and China* (New York: W. W. Norton and Co., 1969), pp. 9f.

5: Satan versus Satan

1. William Manson, *The Gospel of Luke*, The Moffatt New Testament Commentary (London: Hodder and Stoughton, 1930), p. 175.

2. Harrison E. Salisbury, *War between Russia and China* (New York: W. W. Norton and Co., 1969), p. 165; quotes speech by Lin Piao.

3. Houston Peterson, ed., *A Treasury of the World's Great Speeches* (New York: Simon and Shuster, 1954), pp. 710f.

4. *New York Times Book Review*, April 1, 1951.

5. William Manning, quoted in *New Republic*, April 6, 1938, p. 276.

6. E. H. Carr, *Conditions of Peace* (New York: Macmillan, 1943), p. 223.

7. Cited by A. J. Muste, *Not by Might* (New York: Harper and Brothers, 1947), p. 13; cf. Ray Stannard Baker: *Woodrow Wilson: Life and Letters*, 8 vols. (New York: Doubleday, Doran and Co., 1939), p. 582.

8. Peterson, *A Treasury*, p. 726.

9. George Kennan, *Russia and the West under Lenin and Stalin* (Boston and Toronto: Little Brown and Company, 1960), p. 47.

10. Ibid., p. 9.

11. Ibid., p. 32.

12. Ibid., pp. 390f.

13. Pearl Buck, *The Exile* (New York: Reynal and Hitchcock, 1936), p. 155.

14. Ibid., p. 158.

15. Pearl Buck, *My Several Worlds*, cited by James H. Smylie "Fighting Novelist," in *Presbyterian Outlook*, November 4, 1968, p. 5.

16. See *An Unarmed State* (Philadelphia: American Friends Service Committee).

6: Perish by the Sword

1. Gene Lyons, in *New York Times Magazine*, Sept. 18, 1977.

2. Noel F. Busch, *Adlai Stevenson of Illinois* (New York: Farrar, Straus, & Young, 1952), p. 46.

3. E. F. Schumacher, *Small is Beautiful* (New York: Harper and Row, 1973), p. 295.

4. Editorial by Norman Cousins: "Being Healthy is Not Enough," in *Saturday Review*, June 1980, p. 10.

5. Quoted in Fuller Theological Seminary alumni publication, special issue, 1976, p. 5.

6. *New York Times*, April 11, 1977.

7. Ibid., June 10, 1977.

8. Ibid., Dec. 29, 1979.

9. Ibid., April 15, 1980.

10. Ibid., Feb. 29, 1980.

11. Ibid., Sept. 25, 1979.

12. Ibid., March 1, 1976.

13. United Nations Charter: Preamble and Article 11.

14. Norman Cousins, "Manufacturing the News," in *Saturday Review*, June 25, 1977, p. 4.

7: Swords into Plowshares

1. *Development Forum*, January–February 1980, p. 8.

2. *New York Times*, April 1, 1979.

3. Ibid., April 20, 1980.

4. Rolland E. Wolfe, in *The Interpreter's Bible,* 6:897.

5. William Winpisinger, in "Winpisinger Becomes New Sane Co-Chairman," *SANE World*, April 1979, p. 1.

8: The Offering Up of Nations

1. "Letter to Diognetus," in Philip Schaff, *History of the Christian Church*, 7 vols. (New York: Charles Scribner's Sons, 1922), 2:9f.

2. Kenneth Scott Latourette, *History of Christianity* (New York: Harper and Brothers, 1953), pp. 242f.

3. Quoted by Philip van Ness Myers, *Medieval and Modern History* (Boston: Ginn, 1905), p. 125.

4. Roland Bainton, *Church of Our Fathers* (New York: Charles Scribner's Sons, 1941), p. 95.

5. Latourette, *History*, p. 414.

Index of Scriptural Passages

OLD TESTAMENT

121

APOCRYPHA

NEW TESTAMENT